"Shortly after our infant da *written letter from Camilla* ~~and~~ ~~~~ ~~~~ *aching heart. This book captures the heart of that letter."*

—Marjie Canciglia,
mama to Isabella Joy, stillborn, 4/25/13

"Camilla takes the hand of the grieving mother and gently walks her along a path of sorrow she knows first-hand. She bridges the deep chasm of loss with a message of hope; reminding the broken that God will meet them in their deepest despair, carry them in their greatest weakness, and faithfully guide them through the depths of the valley."

—Karen Felmley,
mother of Shepherd Felmley, who went to
the arms of Jesus at 20 weeks gestation

"When we lost our son, James, I felt hopeless and without future. But God has used this book to answer so many of the questions that plagued my mind, and as I saw how He helped her, I experienced healing and hope that only God can give."

—Alanna Soderna,
mother of James, who died at 39 weeks gestation

"Camilla speaks from the heart of a bereaved mother who has experienced unspeakable peace after terrible pain. Her choice of words and the stories she tells are filled with the essence of life—the darker moments and the healing grace she has experienced. Wherever you find yourself on your journey of loss, you have much to gain by reading along."

—Sarah Lee,
mother of Levi Wrangler Lee, who went to the
arms of Jesus at 23 weeks gestation

"Walking alongside her Savior, Camilla Neff tenderly shepherds grieving mothers away from the cliffs of hopeless despair to the safe haven of Christ. Here they can come, in time, to healing and receive His love and grace to grow through the terrible pain into a beautiful giver of comfort and strength. A Bridge of Hope is a priceless resource for grieving parents and those who care for them."

—Marie and Daniel Thomson,
Ceaseless Love Ministries

"As a father who lost an adult son in January 2019, I found myself often nodding my head in agreement. I do recommend this book specifically to moms who lost a child. Honestly, though, this is a good read for anyone who is grieving a loss. Read it. Give it away to a friend in need. You will not be disappointed."

—Dr. Richard Seim, Lead Pastor for 40 years (retired)

"With honesty and faithfulness, this is the true reality of a mother's journey through her world getting shattered. Heartache and yet true beauty are never walked through more delicately than in these pages. This is a must read for all who long for their babe and the dreams they once hoped for."

—Amy Mowery,
mother of Ella Marie and Allie Rae, who went to be with Jesus in the womb; co-founder of the Ella Foundation

"As a mom who has miscarried our first baby, I was touched with Camilla's transparency and her desire to truly help parents through this difficult time. If you're looking for hope in the midst of your pain, this is the book for you."

—Grace Beukema,
mother of Baby "Raphael" Beukema,
who went to be with Jesus at 11.5 weeks gestation

"A remarkably healing book... Both heart wrenching and heart warming, Camilla shares with honesty about her suffering, fears, anger, struggles and healing by God."

—Hongna Fu,
mother of Baby Fu, who went to be with
Jesus at 8 weeks gestation

"A living testimony of the inner torment of a broken heart, the eternal perspective of a purposeful, loving God, clinging to hope unseen, and moving through the broken places to find the triumph of the soul once again. Truly a gift to those who need a helping hand to heal and find life again in the here and now."

—Suzanne Thomson,
Licensed midwife

"I was incredibly blessed to read A Bridge of Hope, having felt the intense heartache of losing two grand babies. If you are seeking encouragement, inspiration and compassion from someone who can completely relate to your pain and walk you through your journey with hope in Christ, then this book is for you."

—Kimberly Stelzer,
grandmother to Kendrah Grace Isitt
and Ian James Isitt, who went to be with Jesus

"Having lost my daughter 5 years ago, A Bridge of Hope offers so much empathy, wisdom, hope and grace for those who have experienced the loss of a child. No matter how short or long it's been, grief will always be there and this book takes you through the endless journey."

—Jenny Ishmael,
mother of Britton Ione, who went to be with Jesus
a few weeks before her due date

"*The warmth with which Camilla shares some of the deepest, most difficult truths God asks us to learn breathes peace and hope to a weary soul. This is a book of sweet comfort and practical guidance for those walking through the overwhelming grief of losing a child.*"

—Sara Jean Smoots,
mother to Baby Smoots, who went to be with Jesus at 7 weeks

"*I'm finding that as I tearfully read every word, I feel closer to Jesus— learning more about His character, how He always carries me in the midst of my suffering with all my raw emotion, longs to heal the broken pieces of my heart, and provides great comfort, allowing my pain to bring about blessing to others.*"

—Autumn Duckworth, doula

"*Written in a devotional style, Neff walks the reader through the deep pain of losing a child, leading them to the true fountain of hope, the Lord Jesus Christ. This book is also a good resource for those who want understanding of those who have experienced loss.*"

—Teletha Elossais,
my mother; also mother to my 4 siblings
who went to be with Jesus in the 1st trimester

"What can you say and do when a child's life is suddenly taken from you or someone you love? This book is far more than the personal and painful experiences of a mom who has walked this road; it is a book saturated with the wisdom from above. As Camilla so eloquently reminds grieving moms, the sun will return and shine upon the bridge that God builds over the hole in your heart."

—Rev. Dr. Daniel W. McManigal,
Hope Presbyterian Church, Bellevue WA

A
BRIDGE
OF
HOPE

Finding Peace in the Pain of Losing a Child

CAMILLA NEFF

Made for Grace
PUBLISHING

PUBLISHING

Made for Success Publishing
P.O. Box 1775 Issaquah, WA 98027
www.MadeForSuccessPublishing.com

Distributed by Made for Success Publishing

First Printing
Library of Congress Cataloging-in-Publication data
Neff, Camilla
A Bridge of Hope: Finding Peace in the Pain of Losing a Child
p. cm.

LCCN: TBD
ISBN: 978-1-64146-395-9 (PBK)
ISBN: 978-1-64146-393-5 (HDBK)
ISBN: 978-1-64146-388-1 (eBK)

Printed in the United States of America

For further information contact Made for Success Publishing
+14255266480 or email service@madeforsuccess.net

A
BRIDGE
OF
HOPE

Finding Peace in the Pain of Losing a Child

CAMILLA NEFF

Dedicated to my first full-term precious baby girl,
Serena Nadine Neff,
who was given an "express ticket" to heaven
on Tuesday, July 28, 2009.

My precious girl, little did I know the plan that God had for your life.

How different it was from the plans and dreams I had for you, but the wonders that God has worked through you have been incomprehensible.

God has used you to change me into a person I would never have been without your life and death. God used you to teach me so many lessons about Him, myself and others—lessons that I would have never been able to understand otherwise.

Your brothers and sisters know a reality that is not common for other children to know, and they have grown up with a greater awareness of the hope that we have because of Jesus.

Your story has brought hope and comfort to many mothers who have also endured the kind of deep pain and anguish that I experienced when I had to say "goodbye" to you. Your little footprints have left a deep mark on my heart, Daddy's heart, your brothers and sisters' hearts, and so many others.

Dear baby girl, you will always be loved and never forgotten.

While I would have loved for you to be here with me, I am beyond grateful that you are enjoying eternal life with Jesus. He has given you a beautiful white robe of His perfect righteousness and you get to enjoy all the glories of heaven. Perfection. Peace. Safety. Jesus' presence.

And so much more.

When Jesus calls my name, I will be coming and we will get to be reunited again for all eternity, never again to say "goodbye."

I love you, Serena!

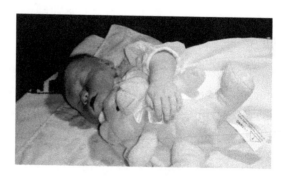

Serena Nadine
"peaceful contented spirit; hope"

Contents

Introduction

At the end of 2015, Amy Mowery, founder of the ELLA Foundation, asked me if I would be willing to write posts for their Facebook page that would give encouragement and comfort to grieving parents. My relationship with Amy began in 2010 when my sister-in-law shared with me that Amy and her husband, Alex, had lost their baby girl, Ella, just days before a scheduled C-section. I had experienced the loss of our first full-term baby girl, Serena, just nine months earlier, and knowing just how deep the pain and anguish are, I reached out to Amy.

Thus began our Internet friendship. We continue to keep in touch today, over nine-and-a-half years later. When she initially asked me to write, I agreed to do so, even if it felt a little unrealistic. I had four little ones who were five-years-old and under, was expecting another blessing in a few months, and I had also begun homeschooling. However, no matter how busy I was, I wanted to bless other grieving parents with the comfort and peace the Lord has given to me as I journeyed this difficult path.

The content in this book is largely born out of the posts that I wrote for the ELLA Foundation bi-weekly. After 18 months of regular posting and the arrival of another precious little one, I decided to take a break from writing. Over time, as I have ministered to several more bereaved mothers and realized that I was sharing many of the same lessons with each one, it seemed as if the Lord was leading me to the idea of publishing the articles. I have a deep desire to reach as many grieving parents as possible; I so desperately want them to be encouraged and be assured, through the things I have learned, that healing will come, comfort can be felt, and peace can be found even in the midst of incredible pain.

From my experience, it seems that the first year is the hardest year—the sting is sharp, and the burden of grief seems more than one can bear. There are so many questions, emotions, and doubts that come with the journey, making life feel like a rollercoaster. We have to learn how to live a "new normal" and come to grips with the reality that all of the dreams, hopes, and plans we had envisioned for the year ahead of us have tragically and dramatically changed.

I have compiled the posts I wrote with the idea that one chapter could be read through each week of the first year, hoping that they can be a little bite to digest every week when the grief is incredibly overwhelming.

Of course, the book is ultimately intended to be read however best serves *you*, whether that means you move slower or faster than I have described. My prayer is that through the readings in this book, you will be met with comfort, hope, and peace through the Holy Spirit.

"Blessed be God, even the Father of our Lord Jesus Christ, the Father of mercies, and the God of all comfort; Who comforteth us in all our tribulation, that we may be able to comfort them which are in any trouble, by the comfort wherewith we ourselves are comforted of God."

—II Corinthians 1:3-4

Mother

"As I have seen a mother bend
with aching, bleeding heart,

O'er lifeless limbs and lifeless
face, so have I had to part

With the sweet prattler at my knee,
the baby from my breast,

And on the lips so cold in death,
such farewell kisses pressed.

"If I should live a thousand years,
time's hand cannot efface,

The features painted on my heart
of each beloved face.

If I should bathe in endless seas,
they could not wash away

The memory of these children's
forms: How fresh it is today.

"Ah, how my grief has taught my
heart to feel another's woe!

With what a sympathetic pang I
watch the tear-drops flow!

Dear Jesus! Must Thou take our lambs,
our cherished lambs away?

Thou hast so many, we so few; canst
Thou not let them stay?

"Must the round limbs we love so well,
grow stiff and cold in death?

Must all our loveliest flowerets
fall before his icy breath?

Nay Lord, but it is hard, is hard,
Oh, give us faith to see,

That grief, not joy, is best for us
since it is sent by Thee.

"And oh, by all our mortal pangs
hear Thou the mother's plea-

Be gracious to the darling ones
we've given back to Thee.

Let them not miss their mother's love,
their mother's fond caress:

Gather them to Thy gentle breast
in faithful tenderness.

"Oh lead them into pastures green,
and unto living springs;

Gather them in Thine arms, and shield
beneath Thy blessed wings.

Ah, little reckon we that weep, and
wring our empty hands;

Blessed, thrice blessed are infant feet,
that walk Immanuel's lands!

"Bless the souls that ne'er shall
know of sin the mortal taint,

The hearts that ne'er shall swell with
grief or utter a complaint!

Brief pangs for us, long joy for them.
Thy holy Name we bless,

We could not give them up to Thee,
Lord, if we loved them less!"

Elizabeth Prentiss

Chapter 1

You Are Not Alone

Dear grieving mother,

I wish I could write this letter specifically to you, knowing your story and the individual facets of heartache that you are going through right now. I understand that everyone grieves differently, and I can imagine you must be going through excruciating pain right now—a pain that you never imagined you would have to endure. You are likely experiencing a whirlwind of emotions ranging from anger, fear, doubt, and disbelief. You may even be feeling that you cannot possibly live with the intensity of such agony.

Whatever place you find yourself as you read, please know that you are not alone. Bereavement is often a lonely journey. Perhaps you have never heard of someone losing their baby, and you feel as if you must be the only one in the world going through this. Perhaps you are in a community that doesn't know how to respond to the needs that you have right now; they don't know what to say or do, so they stay away. Or maybe you've connected with someone who has lost a child, but they grieved differently. In those types of situations, seeing someone else handle sorrow differently sometimes makes us feel like there is something wrong with *us*.

I am writing with the hopes of offering you some encouragement and hope from my own story. Several years ago, I was walking the same path that you are walking now.

My husband and I met in June of 2006. I had met his brother and sister the previous September at a mutual friend's wedding, and when my sisters and I were in the area, we visited their family, and he happened to be there. We hit it off really well—our first conversation lasted five hours, and even then, we could have talked much longer. I lived in Edmonton, Alberta, Canada and he was in Bellevue, Washington, so our relationship was long-distance. We got to know each other through email, and a few visits.

Then, on June 28th, 2008, we were married.

Both of us were eager to begin a family, but we knew the timing was up to the Lord. Needless to say, we were elated when the very next month we discovered that a little one was on the way! Eleven-and-a-half weeks later, our euphoria would come crashing down as I began to miscarry our baby on September 12th. After a weekend of mental torment and self-imposed bedrest in an effort to try to prevent the loss of the baby, I delivered our little baby, who I named "Baby Gad," on Monday, September 15th.

Words cannot even begin to describe how shattered my heart felt during that time. I vacillated between anger and fear, and couldn't understand why God would take away the baby that we had so deeply longed for. It was especially hard knowing we had left our family planning in His hands and had remained pure before marriage. We did everything "right," so why did our baby have to be taken away?

We buried our baby, and when we came back in the house, I felt like something—someone, rather—was missing. Even though the baby had never lived outside of my womb, it had already become a vital part of our family in those eleven-and-a-half weeks—so much so that its absence was felt and deeply missed. I had begun thinking of names, excited for this baby to be the first grandchild for both my parents and my husband's parents, and the first niece/nephew on both sides. The bond between our baby and I had already cemented so much during that brief time. In just one weekend, everything changed.

Thus began the process of God working on things in my heart that needed purging. It felt as if I were enduring open heart surgery on my emotions. Little did I know that it was only the beginning of my surgical intensive and that the process was preparing me for something so devastating it would be almost impossible to comprehend.

The following month, I was blessed to conceive again. I was due on July 17th, 2009, and thanked God for what seemed like beautiful redemption. Though I was overjoyed to know that we were expecting a precious little one once again, I couldn't help but fight fears that maybe I would lose this child as well. While I was still grieving the loss of our first baby, the first trimester was an emotional rollercoaster for me. Any time I didn't feel nausea, I would worry that the baby was lost and a fresh torrent of tears would come rushing down.

With faltering baby steps and a mustard seed of faith, I was starting to learn that trusting God was a daily choice, especially with the things that were most dear to my heart.

As soon as I passed the first trimester, I felt relief from the tremendous anxiety that I battled daily. However, even though it felt like a sigh of relief to be in the second trimester, I still wrestled with fear. When I began to feel our sweet baby move, I would then start to worry when I wouldn't feel any movement. There were no physical reasons to justify my fears—everything always checked out well at my prenatal appointments—but I wrestled a lot with the "what ifs." Finally, one night when I was around six months pregnant, I got out of bed and knelt by the couch. As hot tears streamed down my face, I begged God to keep my baby safe. The fear had almost crippled me. In the dark and stillness of the night, I heard the words in my mind that Jesus had so kindly spoken to Jairus in Mark 5, "Be not afraid; only believe." Those words deeply touched and comforted my heart, and every time I was tempted to worry about the baby, I would remember those words and my heart would be set at ease once again.

We celebrated our 1st anniversary on June 28th and were looking forward to the next month when our little one would finally be born. July 17th came and went with no signs of labor. One week passed, leaving us wondering each day if that would be the day. On July 24th, signs of labor finally began. My contractions were sporadic, but we knew the baby was on its way! Words can't even begin to describe how excited I was! My mother flew into town the next day, and I was like a horse at a starting line, eager for labor to progress so I could meet our darling babe.

We had planned a homebirth with a midwife that had delivered several of my husband's cousins, as well as some of the children of our friends. She was highly recommended, and had over 30 years of experience, having delivered over 700 babies. We felt confident that if anything went amiss, we were in good hands. Worst case scenario, the hospital was just ten minutes away. If something happened, we could race over there, and all would be well.

Consistent labor kicked into high gear around midnight on Sunday morning, and we worked hard at it. The baby's heart rate was always strong and steady; however, the baby wouldn't keep his/her head still so it could mold in the birth canal. It seemed to get caught in the tight muscles inside of me, but I was willing to go through any amount of pain and work tirelessly to bring our baby into the world. Sunday morning turned to Sunday night, and Sunday night turned to Monday. We attempted all kinds of things to help with the labor—different positions, rest times, shower, and more. We tried everything.

My sister-in-law had delivered my nephew just a month earlier, and she had endured a thirty-six-hour labor. She had started in the birth center and was transferred to the hospital when contractions stopped, but my nephew was born alive. We had also heard other stories of first babies taking longer and being harder, so we encouraged ourselves with those thoughts and just kept working at it. With no drop in heart rate, and the baby continuing to move throughout the process, we continued to try with pushing and more pushing.

Finally, my husband saw the baby's head and touched the top of it. We thought it surely wouldn't be that much longer. Even though all signs pointed to delivery, I was both exhausted and swollen. Looking back, I don't think my contractions were strong enough to help me get the momentum needed for those final big pushes. Once again, night came, and I was assured the baby would be here in the morning.

Morning came, the afternoon passed, and the evening was drawing nigh. Shortly after I laid down for a rest, the midwife checked for the heartbeat and could no longer hear it. She got me hooked up to the oxygen machine, and my mother and husband encouraged me to give it my best shot. I was so exhausted and weary that I couldn't do much more than I had already done, and we knew we had to go to the hospital. So, we telephoned them and let them know we were coming.

It was faster to jump in our car and drive ourselves there rather than wait for the ambulance, so we got in and started driving. Much of everything about that drive and getting into the hospital is still a blur to me. We checked in, and when they hooked me up to the machine, they thought that the heartbeat was still there. But, when they performed an ultrasound, they saw that the chambers of the baby's heart were no longer moving. I remember the doctor looking at me in that darkened room and saying the baby was dead. Leaning beside me on the right, my husband immediately broke down in tears, but then he quickly stiffened up and said, "I'm sorry, darling, I have to be strong for you."

I was in total shock and bewilderment, and I was too fatigued to be aware of anything that was going on around me. I needed some alone time, but doctors and nurses surrounded me and decisions had to be made about how we would get the baby out. I begged just to be able to go to the bathroom; anywhere I could be alone for more than a few seconds. While I was in there, with my husband kneeling beside me, I collected my thoughts a bit and braced myself for the task that lay ahead of me: delivering my baby, who was now dead.

In the midst of all of the fog and dark clouds hanging over me, God sent a messenger of peace in the form of nurse, Jeanie, who held my hand and prayed with me. I don't remember what she said, but I distinctly remember looking at her afterward and saying, "I am a Christian too."

Tears rolled down my face as I pushed while the doctor used the "vacuum" (suction cup) to assist in delivering the baby. Nurses on both sides of the bed were holding my hands, and one of them asked if the tears were because of the pain of delivery. In my deep sorrow and pain, I looked up into their faces and said, "It is because I have no living baby on the other side." I can still see that particular moment in my mind and feel the heartbreak as I shared the real reason for my tears with them. I was willing to endure any sort of pain to bring my baby into the world, but now there was a pain that was greater than any physical pain I would endure in labor.

It was 11:37 PM on July 28th, 2009 when our precious little baby came out, and it was announced that it was a girl. I had been so sure our baby was a boy (we had left finding out the gender as a surprise). They lifted our beautiful 9-pound, 2-ounce, 20+-inches-long chunky little girl onto my tummy so I could see her and for one moment, it seemed as if everything was perfect.

Here lay my precious baby girl; the child that I had asked God for and carried for forty-one weeks. Here was the baby that I had prayed for, sung to, talked to, and urged to know who Jesus was and the importance of trusting Him. Here was the baby that I had told so often that knowing Jesus was the most important thing in the world. Here was the baby that I would tell every night, "Goodnight Boubou; Daddy loves you, Mommy loves you, and Jesus loves you too." Every time I said those words, she would slowly wiggle around as if to find the perfect spot and sleep for the entire night. Here was the baby who was the first full-term grandchild for my parents, and the first niece for my siblings.

Shortly after they laid her on my tummy, reality crashed down around us. I was so weary and fatigued; I couldn't even find the tears to cry. I held her and fell asleep—a desperate type of sleep. I have photos of me cradling her in my arms with both of our eyes shut: her with the sleep of death and me with the sleep of the sorrowful. Then I would wake up, and the harsh reality would hit all over again. It was real. I tried to smile for the photos just because that's what you do, right? But, how could I? They wanted to keep me in the hospital overnight, but I just wanted to go home. I needed to escape. I needed a place to really grasp what just happened to me. My whole world had shattered. This wasn't a dream; my worst nightmare had just become a reality.

I remember thinking that I would see her again. I had never experienced something like this before, and I just assumed I would see her when they transferred her from the hospital to the funeral home. So I didn't even think of saying goodbye as I was leaving the hospital. Jeanie asked me if I wanted to, and in all of my foggy thoughts and shock, I thought I would do so even though I would see her again. I whispered goodbye to her, telling her that I loved her. I can still see her lying there in the dark room, bundled in the little baby bassinet as I left. Had I known that was the last time I would see her, I would have held her tightly, kissed her, and really taken advantage of those moments. But I didn't know, and I was still desperately trying to process what just happened to me.

We went home, and I fell asleep almost immediately. I remember waking up the next morning and feeling the sun shining brightly through the windows of our little basement suite. I felt miserable. I went to the bookshelf to get the name book off of the shelf as tears coursed down my cheeks. My mom was sitting on the couch and noticed the tidal wave of emotion threatening to take over.

"What's wrong?" she asked gently.

"I just didn't think I would need this again," I replied, choking back tears.

Could we give our baby the name, Nadine Renae, that we had chosen as an option for a girl? We decided we would choose a different name. When she came out and they put her on my tummy, she looked so peaceful and calm, as if she was looking up into Jesus' face. As the memory flooded back, it became clear to us: we would name our precious little baby, Serena Nadine, which means calm, peaceful and contented spirit; hope.

The next several days were a blur for me. After enduring such a long, arduous labor, my husband's family was solely focused on allowing me time to recover. However, I couldn't stay home while my sisters were going to pick out the flowers that my older sister would use to make the wreath for the casket. I was determined to go, despite their protests. It wasn't easy for me physically. I remember beginning to feel the after-birth effects and having to pace myself. My husband took care of the burial and funeral arrangements. Meanwhile, I was trying to deal with all of the emotions and heart pain that was threatening to overwhelm me.

My dad and siblings were driving down from Canada so the funeral would need to be sooner rather than later. I remember waiting for the funeral and burial to be over, longing for peace and quiet. We buried her on Monday, August 3rd, 2009. I didn't know how I would face the people who would be there. Some close friends, family, and a couple of employees attended the burial. There isn't much that I remember, but I do distinctly recall sitting there under the awning, waiting for the car to arrive with her casket. My husband and father went to retrieve it with my older sister close behind. She carried the beautiful wreath of silk flowers that she had made to lay on top of the casket. I can still see my husband and father carrying the little white casket that had the body of our little girl in it. The pastor spoke some words, and we sang a few songs— two of them being the ones that I would always sing to her while she was growing in my womb. The pastor also chose a version of Psalm 90, and at the time, I couldn't understand how we could sing that song. It didn't seem to resonate with me because of the deep, turbulent emotions in my soul. But years later, it has become one of the dearest songs to me.

> *"O God, our help in ages past, our hope for years to come, Our shelter from the stormy blast, And our eternal home."*

I don't remember if it was then that my husband, Elliott, got up, and I stood beside him, looking at the ground the entire time, burdened by the weight of grief, or if my father and husband lowered her little casket into the hole in the ground. Elliott began to scoop up loads of dirt with the shovel and toss them on top of the casket. After he had scooped several, my father came and took the shovel. I wondered what was going through his mind as he was burying his first granddaughter. My younger brother, who was not even ten-years-old at the time, walked over and took the shovel. It broke my heart to see him scoop up shovelful after shovelful and toss it with such determination on the casket of his first niece. I still tear up thinking about it. And there was my youngest brother, who was five-years-old, standing there with a bouquet of flowers. What was he thinking? He had prayed for this baby. What would his thoughts be about God's answers to prayers? All of my sisters were there too, grieving alongside me, though my pain was so great I didn't notice at the time. Afterward, we went to a church building for a small reception. Looking back, I wish we could have done more to make it a special day, to truly commemorate our daughter, but the shock had paralyzed us and left us reeling.

Driving home after the reception, all I wanted was peace and quiet. I climbed into bed in the middle of the afternoon and couldn't believe that this had all happened to me. I had to start picking up the million pieces that my heart had shattered into, but where could I even begin? I felt as if my heart had a literal hole in it. The pain was so excruciating I didn't know how I could even live. Day after day, I just wept. I cried so much I had no tears left. There were the days where the tears flowed silently, and then there were the days where the "big, ugly cry" emanated from the depth of my being, taking over my entire body.

It was the kind of cry where I wanted to run to a big, grassy field where no one would hear and double over, screaming all of the pain out of every cell of my body. Screaming until I had no voice left. Screaming until I had no more strength left. I endured night after night of traumatic dreams, hearing voices yell, "Push, push, push!" and feeling the weight reverberate through my cells. I also didn't realize that I would need to face all of the physical aspects of postpartum, except I didn't have a baby to go through it with me. My milk came in, and I had to deal with the pain until my body realized it didn't need to produce it—there was no baby to nourish.

My muscles ached in several places from the intensity of the delivery. As my organs shifted back into place, my mind would go back to those wonderful movements that I would feel every day from my precious baby. Then, reality struck. It wasn't my baby.

I stayed indoors most of the time. I wanted to hide. I didn't want to face the questions from others. How could I tell them my story? I felt like a failure. There were so many who had wondered about our decision to have a homebirth, and yes, the length of the labor seemed ludicrous. But we had trusted the expertise of our midwife, and I didn't want to have to try to justify why we hadn't gone to the hospital along with everything I was going through.

As if all of this wasn't enough, there were complications with the suturing. The doctor hadn't done an adequate job, and I dealt with the repercussion of that. I cried out to the Lord, "Why? Isn't the loss of my first baby enough? Now my baby girl gets taken from me too, and I have to deal with this?!" Looking back, things could have been a lot worse, but in the moment, it was just another trial to endure amidst the searing loss I was experiencing.

Days turned into weeks, and weeks turned into months. The leaves changed their colors, and I remember not being able to believe that it was already autumn. My heart was still back in July. Time had stopped for me on July 28th.

In October, I attended a two-day women's conference at a church in Renton, and what a blessing it was for me! It was certainly painful, but it was what I needed to heal. The sessions focused around "strength for life's struggles," and Mary Esvelt shared the lessons she learned through the tragedy that had struck their family when their son was in a terrible car accident, leaving him in a vegetative state. I could identify with so many of the questions and struggles that she had experienced and I learned many rich lessons from her. I have included more on this in the Personal Questions and Answers section at the back of the book.

In November, I found out that we were expecting another baby. It would be due on July 9th, 2010. I was overwhelmed with joy to have conceived again, but the deep pain of losing Serena was still there daily. I was afraid that I might lose this child, too. I remember being on a bus in California, as I had accompanied my husband for a business conference, leaning my head against the window and silently praying that the Lord would keep this baby safe. On the flight back home, I began to miscarry the baby at five-and-a-half weeks. By November 8th, I knew the baby was gone. I felt like my heart was being ripped clean out of my chest. It was as if a dagger was plunged over and over into my heart.

In some ways, this loss was even more painful than the first two. I just couldn't comprehend why this baby was taken away from us after losing our first two babies. Writhing in pain, I asked, "Lord, You took my 1st baby. You took my 2nd baby, and now You have taken another baby? When will it ever be enough?" I named that little baby Ezekiel, which means "the Lord is my strength." The only way that I could pick up and keep going was through the strength of the Lord.

It has been nearly ten years now, as I write. So much has happened, and so many lessons have been learned.

Has the pain lessened? Yes.

Do I ever forget? No.

I want you to know that you are not alone and you *will* make it through. You may be feeling emotions that you never believed were humanly possible. There were so many things I felt that I was embarrassed to tell anyone besides my husband, as I was a Christian. I learned that God's grace and faithfulness were much greater than anything I was feeling. Though that is true, it doesn't take the agony away.

Right now, you may be struggling to keep your head above water, and you may feel like there is no light at the end of the tunnel. I assure you there is, even when you can't see or feel it yet. Jesus promises us incomprehensible peace when we fix our eyes on Him.

We actually chose the verse that speaks to that on Serena's burial stone:

> *"And the peace of God which passes all understanding shall keep your hearts and minds in Christ Jesus."*
>
> —Philippians 4:7

Yes, there is a peace that passes all understanding. And it can be yours. It really can.

"For we have not an high priest which cannot be touched with the feeling of our infirmities, but was in all points tempted like as we are, yet without sin. Let us therefore come boldly unto the throne of grace, that we may obtain mercy, and find grace to help in time of need."

—Hebrews 4:15-16

Chapter 2

Jesus Cares and He Weeps for Our Pain

"Jesus wept."

—John 11:35

The shortest, yet one of the most meaningful verses in the Bible.

As a child, someone would ask me what the shortest verse in the Bible was, and I would smile and quickly answer, "Jesus wept." It was more of a pop-quiz verse to me; something lighthearted. But after we lost Serena, it took on a more profound meaning.

For those of you who don't know the background of this verse, let me explain. In John 11, Jesus' friend Lazarus was very sick, and his sisters had sent a message to Jesus, asking Him to come because they knew Jesus could heal. Jesus delayed in coming, knowing that He had a special plan for the lives of these dear friends. After Lazarus died, Jesus made His way to Bethany, the town where the family resided. Jesus converses with Martha, one of the sisters, and asked where her sister was. Mary, the other sister, comes out to see Jesus, followed by many friends who had come to mourn and weep with her. When Jesus sees her friends and her weeping, the Bible tells us, "He groaned in the spirit and was troubled, and said, 'Where have ye laid him?' They said unto Him, 'Lord, come and see.'" At this point, our verse comes: "Jesus wept." Then said the Jews, "Behold, how He loved him!"

This story became a very comforting one for me after we lost our baby girl. Jesus loved this little family greatly, and yet, that did not mean that they were exempt from tragedy or devastation. It didn't mean that trouble and sorrow would never hit their home. Furthermore, Jesus also had the power to heal Lazarus immediately, whether He was present there in Bethany or whether He would just speak a word or will it from afar (as He healed the centurion's servant). But He had a different plan.

When He first heard that Lazarus was sick, He said, "This sickness is not unto death, but for the glory of God, that the Son of God might be glorified thereby." (John 11:4) Lazarus did end up dying, but Jesus knew that He would raise him from the dead. God would be glorified by the death and resurrection of Lazarus through Jesus' power. But, in order to be raised from the dead, Lazarus would have to die. There would be deep sorrow, pain, heartache and grief for Martha and Mary. Their friends would experience sadness alongside them as they watched his sisters grieve. There may have been anxiety on the part of the sisters as to who would take care of them now with no husbands, no father, and no brother. How would they be provided for in a society where women were not employed?

Another thought of comfort that touched my heart deeply was the fact that the Son of God wept when He saw Mary and the friends mourning even though He knew that He would raise him from the dead. Christ could have come to Bethany all happy-hearted, acting as if there was nothing to worry about because He was in control and He would work a miracle. He could have scolded them for not rejoicing in the fact that God was in control and that they would see their brother again in heaven. He could have asked them why they weren't trusting in God's goodness or reminded them that we are all made of dust and will return to dust; that this is the common lot of all mankind because of our sin. He had every right as the Son of God to do so. But, instead, His heart was tender, loving, and kind. He saw them weeping, and His spirit was troubled. He groaned because of their sorrow and pain. And, He wept. He didn't just shed a silent tear or two.

He **wept**.

I often wondered what it was like for the Father and Jesus when they saw my pain and heartfelt weeping; the agony of my soul and anguish of heart after we lost our baby girl; when they saw my body racked with sobs and the sorrow pouring forth from the deepest part of my being; when there were many nights of silent sobbing and the headache that ensued because of the torrent of tears. While there are no tears in heaven, it comforted me to know that Christ wept on earth when He saw the pain of His loved ones caused by the death of another. When I started to feel the heaviness overwhelm my heart, I simply remembered this story. Each time, I felt a peace wash over my heart, and a sense of calm in His presence surrounded me.

I hope that this account of Christ's interaction with His friends will minister to your heart as it did to mine and give you a deeper understanding of Christ's love for you. Maybe you are questioning whether Christ loves you since He allowed your little one to be taken away from you. Maybe you are questioning whether God sees, and whether He is really concerned with the sorrow of heart that you have on this earth. Maybe you are bitter because there is a happy ending to this story—Lazarus was raised from the dead—but your child still lies in the ground. You may be wondering how God can be glorified through your story since there was no miracle for your child.

Dear one, I assure you that you are not alone in these thoughts and feelings. I will write more about that later, but for today, I pray that you can take comfort in the fact that Jesus, the Son of God, entered into the sorrow of His earthly friends and He wept when He saw their sorrow, grief, and pain. May this knowledge bless you today as you walk through this dark valley. In the darkness that you feel, may it be a glimmer of light.

"And He said unto me, My grace is sufficient for thee: for My strength is made perfect in weakness. Most gladly therefore will I rather glory in my infirmities, that the power of Christ may rest upon me."

—II Corinthians 12:9

Chapter 3

God Has a Special Plan for Your Story

In the last chapter, I spoke of how you may be experiencing bitterness because the ending to your story was not like Lazarus' ending. Jesus had said that Lazarus' sickness was not unto death but that God would be glorified through it all. Lazarus died initially, but Jesus raised him from the dead. His death wasn't the end of his story.

You might be wondering why that happened for Mary and Martha, but it didn't happen for you. You might wonder how the Lord can be glorified when your child's body is lying in the grave, and your heart is bleeding.

Seeing the good that can come out of tragedy definitely doesn't happen overnight, nor in just a couple weeks, or months. It can take years to begin to see how the Lord can bring blessings through the trials and sorrow that come to His people. Regardless of whether it takes six months or several years, I am confident that God will take what the enemy intended for evil and turn it around for good.

In my story, after a miscarriage, a stillbirth, and another miscarriage, I wondered how the Lord would be glorified when all I seemed to birth were dead babies. I had always desired to have a large family, being committed to raising them for His glory and training them to be a light in this world. But this dream was dying quickly with the loss of each baby. The Lord had to bring me to realize, and believe, that He could glorify Himself in whichever way that He chose. He could glorify Himself with the dead children that I bore just as much as He could through living children. He could glorify Himself through a miracle in saving our children's lives and bringing them safely through birth, or He could glorify Himself with allowing them to have an "express ticket to heaven." I needed to trust Him; to trust that He had a perfect plan even though I could not understand it, and to believe that He would be glorified through the pain, sorrow, and even my weakness.

As the months wore on and the years have passed, He has shown me how He can glorify Himself through the death of our little ones. He demonstrates His power to heal broken hearts and to give peace in the midst of turmoil and tragedy. He demonstrates His unconditional love as we grapple with questions, doubts, fears, anxieties, and anger. He demonstrates His longsuffering and patience as it takes us a while to learn the lessons He is trying to teach us. He demonstrates His peace that passes all understanding. He shows us what is hiding in the deepest recesses of our hearts and reveals just how much we need a Savior. He blesses and encourages others as they watch us become stronger in Christ and more like Him as He burns away the dross. They are able to see more of the reflection of Christ in our life as He chips away the stony parts of our hearts. Through the pain and sorrow, He changes us, and through all of that, He is glorified.

If you are struggling with the outcome of your situation, wondering why there was no miracle laid out for you, I pray that the Lord would comfort your heart with the knowledge that He has an even bigger miracle that is in process right now. It is hard to see it through all the tears and anguish, but keep clinging to Him, and little by little, you will see that miracle. Soon you will see Him being glorified through what seems an impossible situation.

Chapter 4

One-Month Birthday

Dear grieving mother,

One month has gone by. As I think back to the first days after we lost Serena, I remember how hard it was to believe it had been a month already. In some ways, it was unbelievable, and in other ways, it seemed like forever since I had held her in my arms, touched her hands and feet, or kissed her. The ache and longing for her was still so intense, and every day was filled with tears. I remember feeling like I was walking around with a gaping hole in my heart, wondering if that feeling would ever go away.

For you, dear mother, your body bears the marks that show you have nurtured a little one within and you are feeling all of the changes that we undergo after a labor and delivery, but your arms are empty. Maybe you have even been asked by a total stranger if you were pregnant, as all of the extra weight hasn't "fallen off." I remember being afraid that someone would ask me that question in the grocery store, resulting in me uncontrollably bursting into tears.

Perhaps you had a lot of support from friends and family in those few first days and weeks after your little one died, but now everyone has started going back to their own lives and routines, and you are struggling to find that "new normal." Day after day, you just don't feel like moving on. Time stopped for you the day of your loss.

You may feel like "hibernating" and hiding. I most certainly felt like hiding away and not facing all of the questions and blank faces.

I hope that today, you will feel the arms of Jesus around you, holding you close and wiping away the tears of pain and sorrow from your eyes. I hope that in the struggle and amidst all of the questions, you will know that He truly cares for you and that He truly does love you.

"But now thus saith the Lord that created thee, O Jacob, and He that formed thee, O Israel, Fear not: for I have redeemed thee, I have called thee by thy name; thou art Mine. When thou passest through the waters, I will be with thee; and through the rivers, they shall not overflow thee: when thou walkest through the fire, thou shalt not be burned; neither shall the flame kindle upon thee."

—Isaiah 43:1-2

Chapter 5:

"Why Me?"

Have you ever asked, "Why me?" Have you ever looked around and found that everything seems to be going just perfectly well for everyone else when all you seem to face is devastation? Have you ever wondered if you were doing (or did) something wrong, and now you're being punished for it? If this is the case for you, have you also wondered how everyone else appeared to get by with the things that you don't feel are permissible? Why are *you* the one that seems to be getting punished?

I remember struggling with these kinds of feelings and more after I miscarried our first baby at eleven-and-a-half weeks. I watched a couple come into the registry office to get a marriage certificate with four children in tow, two of which appeared to be a set of twins that the father was bouncing on his knee while the mother was getting the documents. With it only being a short time since I had lost our baby, the pain was still very raw. As my husband and I drove away, the tears flowed down my cheeks. "Why me, Lord?" I asked. My husband and I had been pure before marriage. We were willing to receive as many children as the Lord would give us. I was prepared and eager to raise a large family for the glory of God. Being a mother was my childhood dream, and in one moment, it was all shattered. I couldn't understand why that couple was given four children and mine was taken away from me.

I also thought about all the babies that were aborted year after year. Why were those babies given to mothers/parents that didn't want them, and the babies that were given to me were taken away from me? That didn't seem fair or just at all. I remember wishing that one day I would open my door to find an unwanted baby sitting there, waiting to be loved. I dreamed of lavishing all of my motherly feelings on it.

Not even a year later, with deeper pain and greater anguish, I again faced the same question when we lost Serena. As I looked at the smiling faces of others who were having their babies within weeks of Serena's death, I wondered why I couldn't have my baby in my arms and they could. In my mind, I could compile a list of all the reasons why I should have been able to keep mine and why they were less qualified to keep theirs.

Just a few months later, I would again be facing this same question when I miscarried our 3rd child at five-and-a-half weeks. "Why me, Lord? Why me?" Wasn't it enough that I had already lost two babies while some women never experienced a miscarriage and actually complained when they conceived "on accident"?

After my first miscarriage, the study I was going through at Bible Study Fellowship was on the Life of Moses. I would have never guessed how deeply God would minister to me through the suffering that the Israelite families were experiencing back then.

Pharaoh was afraid of the people of Israel—their population was skyrocketing, and he was afraid that they would band together with enemy nations and overcome Egypt. So, he enslaved the people. But the more he oppressed them, the more they increased. He made an edict to have all of their baby boys killed at birth but allowed the baby girls to live. As we now know, that plan didn't work. The midwives feared the Lord and wouldn't obey Pharaoh's command, so he resorted to having the baby boys thrown into the Nile River.

Around that time of unrest, Moses was born. His parents observed something extraordinary about him, so they hid him. For three months, it worked, but as he grew older, it was getting hard to conceal him. So, his mother wove a basket, placed him in it, and set him among the reeds in the river. His older sister, Miriam, was instructed to watch to see what would happen. The daughter of Pharaoh came down to the river to bathe and saw the basket. She asked her maids to fetch the basket, and when she opened it, she realized Moses was an Israelite baby. He was crying, and she had compassion for him. Miriam approached her and asked if she would like her to get an Israelite woman to nurse the baby for her. Pharaoh's daughter agreed, and Miriam went to get her mother, Jochebed. Her mother came, and Pharaoh's daughter asked her to nurse him and take care of him. She even offered to pay her! Once Moses was weaned, he would be taken to the palace to become the son of the Pharaoh's daughter.

What an amazing story of deliverance and preservation, right? It seems like the perfect story with the perfect outcome. But, what I realized that year after miscarrying is that not every mother had a perfect outcome. In fact, Jochebed is likely the *only* mother who had that sort of outcome. How many mothers had their baby boys ripped from their arms to be thrown into the Nile River, eaten by crocodiles, or drowned? How many mothers went through labor wondering if they would get to keep their baby? How many mothers feared having a boy because he would be mercilessly killed? How many mothers' and fathers' hearts were torn apart as they were missing a member of their family? Who knows how many they had to give up to death at that point?

It was easy for me to imagine what it would be like if I was Jochebed's neighbor; if my baby boy was thrown into the Nile while she was free to keep hers and paid to nurse her son!! And if that wasn't enough, he would eventually go to the palace and become Pharaoh's daughter's son! I would be outraged, I'm sure.

And then, it was like a lightbulb went off in my mind—a lesson I would have to come back to, time and time again: *God doesn't deal with us in a cookie-cutter fashion.*

The concept sounds very simple, but it is difficult to grasp and accept. God has a unique purpose and plan for each and every person in this world, and what He does in one person's life, He doesn't do in another. He gives to each of His children precisely what we need in order to fulfill that purpose and bring glory to His name here on this earth. For some, it might be through bereavement. For others, it might be through the loss of a job, possessions, status, or health. I am certain that even though you may not see those around you suffering in the same manner, they are likely suffering to some degree you may never see.

I think of how we parent our children in the same manner. Some need work in certain areas, like reading and writing, while others don't. Some are strong-willed, while others are more compliant. As parents, we tailor our instruction, discipline, and training to the needs of the particular child, and so it is with the Lord. He doesn't deal with all of us in a cookie-cutter fashion. He tailors the suffering, pain, discipline, instruction, and blessings to each of us so that through it all, we may be made more like Him and bring glory to His name.

I also thought of the parable of the talents, where one man was given five talents, another two, and another one. The master wasn't looking at how much they were given, but rather he was taking account of what they had done with it. The one with two doubled his talents, while the one with five talents also doubled his. The fact that one had four talents as a result while the other had ten didn't matter: They all received the same approbation/commendation. It wasn't a matter of what or how much was given, but rather what was done with that which was given to them.

And so through both the story of Moses and the parable of the talents, I realized that God doesn't call me to compare my lot in life—the situations, the circumstances, the challenges, the trials, the suffering that I go through—with the lot of others. Rather, He calls me to be faithful with what He has given me. And as a loving Father, He has only planned just what is best for me. Yes, I will not understand it a lot of the time. In fact, I may *never* understand why He chose this path and lot for me. But, choosing to take what He has planned for me and using it for His glory and the benefit of others will be fulfilling His purpose for me and will be a sweet offering unto Him.

"For I know the thoughts I think toward you,"
saith the Lord, "thoughts of peace and not
of evil, to give you an expected end."

—Jeremiah 29:11

Chapter 6

Replacing "Why Me?" with "Why Not Me?"

In the last chapter, I spoke of my struggle with the question, "Why me?" and how I had to learn that God does not deal with His children in a cookie-cutter fashion. He tailors everything to our specific inclinations, needs, and His perfect plan for our lives.

This next part might sting quite a bit, but it was an essential part of me learning to overcome this question that kept plaguing me.

Are you ready?

I had to learn to ask the question, "Why *not* me?"

When I stopped looking at others around me and what they had been given, it allowed me to start looking at what I *had* been given. I started looking at what I had been saved from and all the blessings God had given me, despite how many times I fell (and still fall) short of His standards. As I looked back on all the times

He had come through for me in incredible ways, the "Why me?" question started to fade.

Now, don't get me wrong; I know it is terribly hard to do this. You may not feel like counting your blessings right now. You may even feel like doing so would be lying to yourself about how you really feel. But I encourage you, dear mother, take all of those things to Jesus. Tell Him that you simply don't feel like looking at all your blessings. Tell Him that you would give so many of your other blessings if only you could have your precious baby. Tell Him you want to be made like Him, but it is incredibly challenging to look at this from His perspective. Ask Him to give you His eyes to see the bigger picture. Ask Him to help you to trust even when you can't understand why it happened to you.

In my life, after I confessed where my heart was really at, I would bathe my mind with all the stories of the saints of old who had terrible things happen to them. I asked myself how they could have asked the same question in their own circumstances: "Why me?"

Joseph: sold as a slave.

David: running for his life because of Saul's jealousy.

Daniel: thrown to the lions.

Jeremiah: in the slime pit.

Job: losing everything he owned and all his children in one day.

Thankfully, we know the end of these stories. We know that God had great things planned for them and that it is often the hardest and most painful things that we go through which cause the greatest things to be worked in and through us.

Dear friend, know that even now, when you feel as if there is no end to your pain, Jesus loves you so much that He is going to use this suffering to do something great. I must confess there were days when I honestly didn't care about the bigger picture and the greater plan God had. But even then, His hands held me and gently brought me back to having a heart for His will.

I know this might have been a lot to take in, so I will stop there for now. I sincerely hope and pray I didn't add to your pain by anything I wrote. Please forgive me if I have. My hope in sharing this is that some of the most painful lessons I had to learn will be a help to you as you go through this grievous trial. I liken these painful lessons learned through suffering to cleaning out an infected wound. If we leave the infection in the wound, it gets worse and worse, increasing our pain and threatening to overcome our body. In the worst of cases, the infection may end up killing us. But if we are willing to allow the Surgeon to open up the wound, drain all the pus, and then soothe it with His healing balm of truth, while it initially hurts terribly, we ultimately gain relief from the pain, and we begin our journey to healing. We must endure the greater pain in order to find relief that lasts.

I do encourage you to take your questions, anger, and frustration to Jesus. Pour them out at His feet. Be open and honest with Him, telling Him how you feel it isn't fair, that it doesn't seem right and that you don't understand how this aligns with a perfect will. Whatever it looks and sounds like, lay it all out before Him. I found when I was perfectly honest with Christ, He would bring to remembrance things I learned in Scripture, heard in past sermons, or read in books. I believe He will do the same with you.

Pray for ears to hear what He wants to say and pour out your broken heart today.

> *"Trust in Him at all times; ye people, pour out*
> *your heart before Him: God is a refuge for us."*

—Psalm 62:8

Jesus loves you so much. He truly does care deeply about your pain, and I promise He will carry you through.

"When I thought to know this, it was too painful for me; Until I went into the sanctuary of God; then [I] understood..."

—Psalm 73:16-17

Chapter 7

Why Does It Have to Be the Loss of My Child to Teach Me a Lesson?

You might be wondering, "God, why does it have to be the loss of my child? I know You say that You can use all things for Your glory and my good. I know that there are wonderful lessons You can teach me through whatever You allow in my life, but why did it have to be the loss of my child? Am I so terribly stubborn that it has to be *this*? Why couldn't You have chosen something else to teach me these invaluable lessons that people are telling me I will learn through suffering?"

Oh, dear mother, I asked myself these very same questions. I have to say that for myself, children are the area that will strike at the very core of my being. With other kinds of suffering, I can generally take it in stride and use all of the Scriptures I can find on suffering to bolster my spirits, standing strong and valiant through the trial. But losing a child? Several children? That is a different story. Looking back, I know that if it weren't through losing a child,

I wouldn't have learned the lessons I did (and to the degree that I learned them).

You may not feel that way. And perhaps if you do, it still doesn't offer any soothing balm for your pain. That is OK. God can meet you right where you're at.

Perhaps thinking of the many Bible characters in Scripture who underwent suffering will help us to gain the Lord's perspective. I am sure that they may have thought of different paths God could have led them down in order to learn the lessons He had planned for them. I think of David—having to run for his life from Saul, living as a fugitive for years, away from his wife, his family, and his closest friend, Jonathan. He had to stay away from the established worship place of God, too. I am sure he wondered why his road to being the King of Israel included all of that. Why didn't God just cause Saul to die in his sleep or in a battle with the Philistines, and then Samuel announce that David was God's choice for the next King of Israel? That would have been a lot more comfortable and include a significantly less amount of suffering and pain. But would David have known the profound spiritual truths that he learned if the path to the kingdom was different? How was God equipping him for his position of authority and ruling the kingdom of Israel by everything he suffered while running for his life from Saul? What kind of deep character was drilled into his being because of what he experienced? How much did his relationship with God deepen and strengthen because of the suffering he underwent?

Speaking of drawing encouragement from the believers in the Bible who underwent suffering, one day, I was studying the opening chapter of 1 Samuel, and it begins with the story of Hannah. Hannah is barren. Peninnah, her husband's 2nd wife, provokes her and vexes her, reminding her that she is barren and Peninnah has a "tribe" of children. Hannah pours her heart out to the Lord, making a vow to dedicate her son to the Lord if God gives her a son. The Lord answers her prayer within a short time, she conceives, bears a son named Samuel, and Hannah fulfills her vow.

Once again, there is deep suffering to be seen in this story. I am sure Hannah couldn't understand why she was barren. After all, Peninnah was the one with terrible character, arrogantly vexing Hannah because she was prolific, and Hannah didn't even have one child. How long did Hannah have to endure that pain? We don't know exactly how long, but if Peninnah had at least four children (the verses speak of "all her sons and daughters," so it was likely she had many more than just four), it would have been a minimum of four years. Probably more like six to eight years, maybe longer! Finally, God answered her request and Hannah's son became one of the most famous prophets of Israel. But it didn't stop there: He blessed her with more children. Perhaps Hannah also questioned why it had to be barrenness that she was afflicted with. It was considered a shame in Israel to be barren. We can speculate that could have been why her husband had a 2nd wife—because he wanted to have sons to pass on his inheritance.

As I pondered Hannah's suffering and how she must have felt during the time, I realized something I had never thought of before when considering her story: *I* am gaining hope from the suffering she endured and the miraculous answer that God gave to her. When we are in the midst of a trial, we often keep thinking, "What lessons does God have for me to learn?" But maybe there are lessons He intends for *others* to learn through our suffering. Hannah endured the pain of barrenness and being ridiculed for years. Thousands of years later, we can look at her life and gain comfort that the Lord heard her cries and saw her pain. We glean hope from the fact that He listened to her plea and blessed her with not only one son, but several more children after that.

I can think of many other characters in Scripture whose pain and suffering brought blessing to others as well: Ruth came to faith as she interacted with Naomi and endured the pain of loss with her. The nation of Israel was saved during the famine because of the suffering Joseph underwent. King Nebuchadnezzar and King Darius were blessed with the opportunity to see living faith in action by Daniel, Shadrach, Meshach, and Abednego. The nation of Israel was blessed by the leadership of Moses, who suffered a tremendous amount to lead them out of Egypt and into the Promised Land. Thousands of years later, we are encouraged by the faith and perseverance of these saints through the suffering that they endured.

Most importantly, we can be encouraged through the life of Christ. Remember, Jesus' suffering was not because of His own sin or stubbornness. He suffered so that we could be saved from an eternity in hell. He didn't endure crucifixion because He was stubborn, and He didn't endure crucifixion because He deserved the judgment that had to be inflicted on Him. He suffered for *our* sake. It was all because of His great love for us that He was afflicted so we could be saved from God's wrath. By *His* stripes, we are healed.

Perhaps God has brought the trial of the loss of our precious baby into our lives because He is faithfully working in others' lives as well. Perhaps He is using our story to show others how faithful He is to His people. Perhaps He is preparing them for the trials that they will have to walk through.

As I think about this transforming perspective—that others are benefited by the suffering we undergo—I remember listening to a sermon years ago on audio about suffering. The minister was saying something along the lines of, "Perhaps someone is watching you as you go through your suffering and saying, 'Wow, if that happened to me, I would just forget God and walk away from Him.' But as they see your steadfast commitment to God, your dependence on and your trust in Him, even when you have had your heart broken into a thousand pieces, this is a testimony to them of your faith in God and His goodness to His people."

I hope these things will be a help to you as you grapple with questions that overwhelm your mind day and night. Remember, Jesus loves you. He really does. Hold on to Him. Keep pouring out your heart to Him. He will lift you up on His wings when you are too weary to keep on going.

GOD MOVES IN A MYSTERIOUS WAY

BY WILLIAM COWPER (1774)

God moves in a mysterious way
His wonders to perform;
He plants His footsteps in the sea
And rides upon the storm.

Deep in unfathomable mines
Of never failing skill
He treasures up His bright designs
And works His sov'reign will.

Ye fearful saints, fresh courage take;
The clouds ye so much dread
Are big with mercy and shall break
In blessings on your head.

Judge not the Lord by feeble sense,
But trust Him for His grace;
Behind a frowning providence
He hides a smiling face.

His purposes will ripen fast,
Unfolding every hour;
The bud may have a bitter taste,
But sweet will be the flow'r.

Blind unbelief is sure to err
And scan His work in vain;
God is His own interpreter,
And He will make it plain.

Chapter 8

Two-Month Birthday

Dear grieving mother,

Two months have passed. I am sure that at times it still feels unreal and you are hoping you will wake up and find out that it was all just a horrible nightmare. At the same time, you may be replaying in your mind every moment that you had with your little one, trying not to forget the tiniest detail of those priceless moments.

You may be wondering when the awful sting of grief will go away. It may feel like it worsens as each day goes by. I don't want to discourage you, but it was quite a while before that excruciating pain went away for me. I don't remember exactly when, but it was at least several months... more likely after the 1st anniversary.

I say this to "encourage" you. I know it doesn't exactly sound encouraging, but I just want you to know that you are experiencing something that is normal for those who have undergone the loss of a child and that you *will* get through this. There will come a day when that agonizing, overwhelming pain is no longer searing through your being; when you will be able to think about your little one with a smile instead of tears streaming down your cheeks. Give yourself time, and be patient with yourself. Don't put a timeline on your grief. Face each day, one at a time; each moment at a time. Know that Jesus is right there, carrying you through every day, even when you don't feel like He is.

You may be wondering if you will ever get through this and if Jesus is walking through this deep valley with you. When I struggled with believing the truth that God was with me every step of the way, the story of Shadrach, Meshach and Abednego helped to comfort me when I felt alone.

Just in case you aren't familiar with the story, these three men were Hebrew captives in Babylon. They had proven themselves to be wiser than the other wise men of the realm and were promoted to high positions in King Nebuchadnezzar's kingdom. He decided to build a golden image and required everyone to bow down to it whenever the music signal was given, upon pain of death in the fiery furnace. Shadrach, Meshach, and Abednego refused to do so, enraging the king. He was willing to give them another chance, but they didn't recant. They were ready to be thrown into the furnace rather than deny the only True Holy One of Israel. Nebuchadnezzar was now vehement with wrath and commanded that the furnace be heated seven times hotter. He instructed that they be tied up, clothes and all, and cast into the furnace. The heat was so intense that the soldiers who threw the three men into the furnace were instantly killed from the heat.

But what happened to Shadrach, Meshach, and Abednego? King Nebuchadnezzar looked into the furnace and saw four—not three, but four—men walking around in the furnace, untouched and seemingly unaware of the fact that they were in a raging fire. He asked, "Didn't we throw three men in? Lo, I see four men loose, walking in the midst of the fire, and they have no hurt; and the form of the fourth is like the Son of God." (Daniel 3:25) What a powerful statement from a heathen king, so set upon himself and elevated with pride and conceit! Calling them out of the furnace, Nebuchadnezzar found that they were entirely unharmed; that not one hair of their head was singed, their clothing had not changed, and no smell of fire could be detected on them. It was a complete miracle!

What a testimony that Jesus is right there, in the hottest of fires, walking with us. Right now, you may not feel like He is there, but those looking in at you will be able to see that Jesus is there. They will be able to see Him holding you, carrying you and lifting you up when you are too weak to keep going. Remember that the fires will not harm you, and the smell of smoke will not be detected on you because Jesus is right there with you, walking beside you, holding your hand in the midst of that excruciating furnace.

"He giveth power to the faint; and to them that have no might He increaseth strength."

—Isaiah 40:29

Chapter 9

The Refiner's Fire

"For Thou, O God, hast proved us: Thou hast tried us,
as silver is tried. Thou broughtest us into the net: Thou
laidst affliction upon our loins. Thou hast caused men to
ride over our heads: we went through fire and through
water: but Thou broughtest us out into a wealthy place."

—Psalm 66:10-12

Does it feel like you are in a furnace right now? Does the fire seem so excruciatingly hot, you feel like your skin is melting and dripping off of you? Is the pain so fierce that you feel like screaming in agony? Is your only desire just to get relief from the pain that burns through your soul?

In the days and months following the loss of our Serena, I remember my husband encouraging me with the picture of a refiner. A refiner heats the fire only as much as is needed to burn out the dross, but not too hot that it will destroy the gold. A refiner never takes his eyes off of the gold while it is in the fire. And, best of all, the refiner knows that the gold is pure when he can see his own reflection in it.

As I reflected on these things, a whole new light was shed on those Scriptures that speak of us being refined and God being a Refiner. Oftentimes we feel like this is just too great a trial for us; feeling as if we are literally drowning in grief and sorrow and that there is no way possible that we are going to make it out alive. I found comfort in the fact that the Lord would not heat the furnace hotter than was needed to burn the impurities out of me to make me more like Him. Furthermore, during the entire time of the pain and suffering I was undergoing, He would never take His eyes off of me. He would be there to help me endure, to wipe my tears, and to pick me up when I was so fatigued from the sorrow that I couldn't possibly move forward on my own. Yes, there were days when I felt that He had hidden His face from me; that He had forgotten me in the furnace and that I was left there to die in the searing flames. But, no! Looking back, He kept His eyes on me the entire time I was in that furnace.

Even still, the greatest comfort was that I could look forward to the fact that all of this suffering and pain would not be in vain. It was not just a random act of chance or ill fortune. His aim was to be able to see His reflection in my life. He was using this devastation to make me look more like Him; to transform me into a beacon of light for His kingdom.

Though the furnace experience was far from pleasant, it would yield beautiful results. And the verse noted above gives us hope in the fire: "…but You brought us out into a wealthy place." The furnace will not last forever. God will bring us through it. Though it seems like there is no end in sight, and you feel as if you will never make it through the pain, cling to Christ. Remember that He is in the furnace walking with you, just like He was with Shadrach, Meshach, and Abednego. He will keep you faithful. Cling to Him in faith.

Here is a poem that was read by a pastor whose sermon I listened to online a few years back. I just recently found it online and am comforted by these words to this day. I pray they minister to your heart just as much.

He sat by a furnace of seven-fold heat,

As He watched by the precious ore,

And closer He bent with a searching gaze,

As He heated it more and more.

He knew He had ore that could stand the test,

And He wanted the finest gold

To mold as a crown for the King to wear,

Set with gems of a price untold.

So He laid our gold in the burning fire,

Though we fain would have told Him, "Nay,"

And He watched the dross that we had not seen

As it melted and passed away.

And the gold grew brighter and yet more bright,

But our eyes were so dim with tears;

We saw but the fire – not the Master's hand

And questioned with anxious fears.

Yet our gold shone out with a richer glow,

As it mirrored a Form above

That bent o'er the fire, though unseen by us,

With looks of ineffable love.

Can we think that it pleases His loving heart

To cause us a moment's pain?

Ah, No! but He saw through the present dross

The bliss of eternal gain.

So He waited there with a watchful eye,

With a love that is strong and sure,

And His gold did not suffer a whit more heat

Than was needed to make it pure.

James M. Gray

"...though now for a season, if need be, ye are in heaviness through manifold temptations: That the trial of your faith, being much more precious than of gold that perisheth, though it be tried with fire, might be found unto praise and honor and glory at the appearing of Jesus Christ."

—I Peter 1:7

Chapter 10

Remaining Faithful

*"Ye shall not need to fight in this battle; set yourselves,
stand ye still, and see the salvation of the Lord with you, O
Judah and Jerusalem: fear not, nor be dismayed; tomorrow
go out against them; for the Lord will be with you."*

—II Chronicles 20:17

Does it feel as if every day is a fight? Are you feeling as if you are in a constant wrestle with God? Are you battling thoughts of doubt, fear, bitterness, resentment, and anger? As if that isn't enough, are you fighting the cruel comments from those around you who don't understand, who are trying to be helpful but only pour salt into your throbbing wound? Do you feel like all the demons of hell have been unleashed and the moment you feel like you have triumphed over one, another one appears, and you simply don't have the strength to fight another moment?

Yes, my dear friend, it is a fight. I understand. I have been there.

When we lost Serena during labor after having lost one to a miscarriage before her death, only to lose another to miscarriage after her death, I found myself in all of those scenarios above. It certainly felt like a battle and a battle that I wasn't too good at fighting either. While on the outside, I appeared to be handling my trials wonderfully and was even asked to become a Discussion Leader at my local BSF (Bible Study Fellowship) group, the battle raged inside. The thoughts that were running through my mind at the time were embarrassing for me to reveal, being a Christian. No matter how much I didn't want to be thinking them, they plagued my mind.

It was something I faced daily, sometimes hourly. The thoughts and feelings had to be fought, but there were days when I felt that I couldn't fight anymore. There were days when I felt like I was crawling on my hands and knees, begging Jesus to help me make it through. Here is a poem that I wrote in my journal, dated December 9th, 2009 (four months after losing Serena, and one month after miscarrying Baby Ezekiel).

IT'S ONE OF THOSE DAYS

It's one of those days...

The mask is put on and stays,

Wanting to run away

My burden aside to lay.

But no matter where I go

The pain I'll always know.

The tears will often flow

And my heart will ache so.

It's indescribable- my heart-

I feel like I'm ripped apart.

The wound does sear and smart,

So torn—do I still have a heart?

I see myself there

Face bowed, covered with hair,

The cheeks that once were fair

Worn with burden and care.

Looking up with tears streaming

"Isn't it enough?" in pain I'm screaming.

My knees bending, my eyes pleading,

Cringing in agony as my chest is heaving.

Then bang!

A loud noise clangs!

The echo does hang,

Through me shoots pangs!

I'm begging.

I'm pleading.

I'm sobbing.

I'm grieving.

Then I'm there

Wet face and matted hair,

How much hope do I dare?

Will there be any care?

Then, smack!

Whack!

Turn back and

Another whack!

Through my body pain sears;

My eyes just flood with tears.

All of the demons lift up their jeers

As it all happens- one of my worst fears.

"What is it that You want from me?

I'm trying to be all that I can be.

I'm trying so hard, obediently,

But 'seems like I'm failing miserably.

Tell me, Lord, what have I done?

What will my life ever become?

Why is Your anger waxed so hot?

And sorrow after sorrow has become my lot?

But, Lord, I will love You in times of pain.

Lord, I will serve You in times of rain.

And if You will to give me sorrow again,

Let my love and trust in You never wane."

It's one of those days.

The mask's put on and stays.

I know I cannot run away,

So before the Lord my burden I lay.

I share this poem to both give you a glimpse into the rawness of the pain I was experiencing at the time and to offer some hope that this was how low I had sunk under the burden of grief. How was I able to be lifted out of such mire? As the poem notes, it was through prayer, reading of the Scriptures, and God's immense faithfulness and grace.

During this time, I remember reading the account of Job, and chapters one and two gave me renewed courage and strength to continue the fight.

Job was doing all the right things. He had God's stamp of approval: "Hast thou considered My servant Job, that there is none like him in the earth, a perfect and an upright man, one that feareth God and escheweth evil?" (Job 1:8) What a word of commendation that came from the lips of God! However, Satan then comes and challenges God: "Doth Job fear God for naught? Hast Thou not made an hedge about him, and about all his house, and about all that he hath on every side? Thou hast blessed the work of his hands, and his substance is increased in the land. But put forth Thine hand now, and touch all that he hath, and he will curse Thee to Thy face." (Job 1: 9-11) God then grants Satan permission to do whatever he wants with everything that Job has. But, He gives Satan a limit: He couldn't touch Job himself.

Naturally, Satan takes full advantage of the offer. Can you imagine what it would have been like to be in Job's place? First, it was all the oxen and donkeys taken by the Sabeans; then it was fire from God falling and burning up all the sheep. To make a complete decimation of all of Job's wealth and possessions, the Chaldeans came and took away all the camels. When things didn't seem like they could get any worse, someone ran in with the terrible news that all ten of his children were killed in a natural disaster... just like that. Not one, not two, not half or nine; all of them! Everything was gone in a single day!

Job wasn't aware of the dialogue that had taken place between Satan and God. He didn't know that this was a test. But how did he respond? He arose, tore his clothes, shaved his head and fell down upon the ground and worshipped, saying, "Naked came I out of my mother's womb, and naked shall I return thither: The Lord gave, and the Lord hath taken away; blessed be the name of the Lord." In all this Job did not sin or charge God foolishly. (Job 1:20-22)

As if that wasn't enough, when God again upholds Job's character to Satan (even though Satan had wreaked such havoc in his life), Satan presents God with another challenge: "But put forth Thine hand now, and touch his bone and his flesh, and he will curse Thee to Thy face." Once more, God grants Satan to have power over Job but gives him another limitation: "Save his life." Satan smites Job with sore boils that cover his body. Job's wife comes and tempts him to "Curse God and die." How does Job respond? "Thou speakest as one of the foolish women speaketh. What? Shall we receive good at the hand of God and shall we not receive evil?" In all this did not Job sin with his lips." (Job 2)

As I sat and pondered this in light of my own devastating circumstances at the time, two things really stood out to me and caused me to wonder, *What if Satan challenged God regarding me? Am I going to give in? Am I going to "let God down?" Am I going to betray Him?* As I thought of Satan and his wickedness, a wave of righteous anger and zeal arose within me. I couldn't give in. I couldn't let him win. I couldn't let him laugh in the face of my God; my Savior who had died for me. You see, Satan would have wanted me to give up the fight, to turn my back on God, to prove to God that I wouldn't make it through this trial. But thinking of Satan gaining the victory made me shudder.

Of course, let me be clear: I was only preserved by the grace of God. It was only the work of the Holy Spirit within me that gave me this renewed courage and zeal for the fight. Nonetheless, I was strengthened by our friend Job's loyalty to God despite the grievous circumstances. Whereas moments earlier, I had been at the point of not wanting to fight another battle, now I was donning my armor, once again, using the Sword of the Spirit to fight those fiery darts that so often were shot at me. Once again, I called out for grace to overcome, rather than succumbing to the tactics of Satan.

While we're on the topic of fighting Satan's tactics, I wanted to share some "nuggets," as I call them, from my Bible Study notes regarding warfare that were helpful for me to remember. I pray that you will be encouraged by them as well.

The notes spoke to the fact that suffering is not exempted from the life of those who are committed to Christ. They will indeed experience suffering, but because of His strength, they can rise above the suffering on eagle's wings. Isaiah 40:30, 31 gives us so much comfort as it assures us of the triumph that God's people will certainly have:

"Even the youths shall faint and be weary, and the young men shall utterly fall: But they that wait upon the Lord shall renew their strength; they shall mount up with wings as eagles; they shall run and not be weary; and they shall walk, and not faint."

The Notes also encouraged me, reminding me that, by the power and blood of Jesus, our suffering defeats Satan. As we persevere in the affliction that we face, it is just one more victory over Satan and it inspires other believers to stand strong and persevere.

Furthermore, on this topic of battling Satan, the following verses came to me a couple weeks before I went into labor with Serena, and have been an encouragement to me ever since: "And the Lord said, 'Simon, Simon, behold, Satan hath desired to have you, that he may sift you as wheat; But I have prayed for thee, that thy faith fail not: and when thou art converted, strengthen thy brethren." (Luke 22:31-32)

How comforting it is to know that Jesus has been, and is, praying for us as we walk through this dark valley. How comforting it is to know that He has the power to keep our faith from failing, and how comforting is that promise He gives to Simon Peter: "when." Not "*if* you are converted," but "*when* you are converted." What a beautiful promise! Simon Peter wouldn't fall forever; the battle wouldn't go on forever, he would be victorious in Christ! Then comes the call of duty — to "strengthen your brethren." It is for your sake just as much as it is for the people around you that your faith is strengthened.

It is my hope that you will find comfort in the fact that Jesus is praying for you right now as you walk through this dark time. He is praying that your faith will not fail even if it *feels* like your faith is currently failing. Take heart; He has overcome. The battle is already won!

"It is of the Lord's mercies that we are not consumed, because His compassions fail not.

They are new every morning: great is Thy faithfulness."

—Lamentations 3:22-23

Chapter 11

The Sun Will Shine Again

One morning, when I awoke, the sun was shining through my window with such brilliance, it was invigorating. Living in the Pacific Northwest, we have some long days, and sometimes, weeks of dreary, drizzly weather. As I prayed with the children before we ate breakfast, I thanked the Lord for this radiance of light as I remembered those days after Serena's death when it seemed like there would only be endless "rainy" days: dreary days, gloomy days, days with a cloud over my heart. I often wondered if I would ever be able to truly smile again. The pain in my heart was so real that it felt like I was walking around with a literal hole in my chest. The ache turned into a throb, and I wondered if I would ever be the same. As each day passed, weeks turned into months, and the sorrow continued to cloud everything. I wondered if the "sun" would ever return in my life.

Six-and-a-half years later, I can confidently say that yes, the sun did return. The gloomy, cloudy days became fewer and farther between, and I felt the warmth of God's countenance once again. I can laugh and smile, and the ache doesn't throb anymore. He has given me the oil of joy in place of mourning, and the garments of praise in place of the spirit of heaviness. Of course, there are days when those clouds return and the tears rain down my cheeks; when I want to hold her just one more time, kissing those chubby cheeks and clasping those pudgy hands. There are days when I muse on all the events of the labor and delivery; I wish she was in my arms again and would miraculously open her eyes, staying here with me.

And I believe it might always be that way. I am not sure that one ever "gets over" the loss of a child, and I think that is okay. I consider it the special gift that God gives to us, as parents, to hold their memory so dear to our heart that we still feel that twinge of pain years after they have gone. Someone told me (or I read it, I can't remember which) that in time, there would be a bridge that would be built over the hole in my heart. Though I didn't understand at the time, I can now wholeheartedly agree that this is true.

Whether the bridge has not yet begun to be built over the deep hole in your heart, or whether the rainy days still outnumber the days when the sun peeks out from behind the clouds, it is my hope that you will be encouraged that the Lord *will* allow the sun to shine once again. He *will* build that bridge over the hole in your heart. Be encouraged, dear grieving mother: the clouds will part, and the light will shine forth.

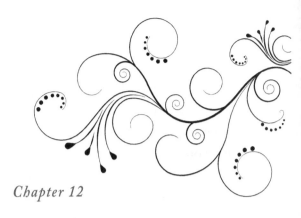

Chapter 12

Three - Month Birthday

Dear mother,

Have three months really gone by? I remember imagining what Serena would be doing at three months: rolling over, smiling at me, having more wake times and sleeping less during the day. My nephew was born the month before Serena, so it wasn't too hard to visualize what she would be doing if she were alive.

Was it difficult to see him? Of course it was.

But even still, I felt that, by facing the reality that he was here and she wasn't, it would help me grieve in the present instead of burying the pain. I knew that it would most certainly haunt me later if I chose to ignore it, so I allowed myself to grieve. I never wanted my little nephew to think that Auntie didn't love him, so I ensured that I demonstrated love and care, even though it wasn't easy. I held him and kissed him, played with him and cuddled him. Several years later, I now see how God used that choice to do the right thing, even when it was painful. He used it to bring much-needed healing to my shattered heart.

⁓

Perhaps you may also be wondering how God can bear with you through all of your weakness, doubt, and anger. Perhaps you are feeling like you are stuck under a cloud of depression. Perhaps you are wishing that you could be stronger under this pain and that you are failing miserably as a Christian. Perhaps you are wondering where your strong faith is that you thought you had, or where the deep relationship with God went that you once had.

Take heart, dear one. You are not alone. I experienced the same emotions and feelings. There were days when I asked the Lord to take me home to heaven because I was failing so miserably at trusting Him in my pain. I felt like I was betraying Him in my heart because I couldn't calm the fears, doubts, and anger that I was feeling. I had no clue if anyone else ever felt these horrible emotions and wondered if I was going to fall away from the Lord. I knew in my head that the Lord will always hold His children in His hands, but when you are in such a dark place, sometimes it is easy to question whether or not you are a Christian.

Can you relate? The devil loves to play games with your mind and torment you beyond measure. The battle is fierce and exhausting, and warfare seems constant. Oftentimes, you feel like you can never get away from it. Death appears to be a welcome relief from all of the mental torment and agony; but even more so, death seems to be a welcome relief because you feel like you are failing the Lord so badly. You just want to go home, free from this sinful flesh and world.

Perhaps that is how Elijah felt. I Kings 18 relates a massive display of God's power on Mount Carmel where the prophets of Baal were put to shame as their "god" didn't answer all of their cries and dramatic displays for fire to come down. On the other hand, Elijah simply prayed quietly, and God answered with fire that not only consumed the offering, but licked up all the water that had been poured on the altar, the water filling the trench around it, and every rock of the altar as well!

After this mighty victory, Elijah is terrified when Queen Jezebel swears to put him to death by the next morning. He had just seen God's mighty, miraculous power; how could he be running for his life the next day? We could say, "Elijah, don't you think that God can save you?" But Elijah was a human just like the rest of us. Often, after "mountaintop experiences," we are faced with "dark valleys." Perhaps Elijah was a little disillusioned. Maybe after such a victorious display on God's part, he thought that Israel would come back to Him and the king and queen would be convinced as well. When that didn't happen, he may likely have been caught off guard. We can imagine he may have been deeply discouraged, wondering if the nation of Israel would *ever* come back to God. But, getting more to the point, when he heard the news from Jezebel,

> *"...he arose, and went for his life, and came to Beersheba,*
> *which belongeth to Judah, and left his servant there. But*
> *he went a day's journey into the wilderness, and came and*
> *sat down under a juniper tree: and he requested for himself*
> *that he might die; and said, It is enough; now, O LORD,*
> *take away my life; for I am not better than my fathers."*
>
> —I Kings 19:3-4

Can you relate? I definitely could. I felt like I was failing miserably, wondering what use my life would be for the Lord. I was finding it challenging to trust Him and to surrender my will to His. I felt that my light had been snuffed out, so what was the point for

me to live and be a blot on God's name? But how did God respond
to Elijah's discouragement and emotional fatigue?

> *"And as he lay and slept under a juniper tree, behold, then
> an angel touched him, and said unto him, Arise and eat.
> And he looked, and, behold, there was a cake baken on the
> coals, and a cruse of water at his head. And he did eat and
> drink, and laid him down again. And the angel of the LORD
> came again the second time, and touched him, and said,
> Arise and eat; because the journey is too great for thee."*

—I Kings 19:5-7

What loving kindness of the Lord!

He didn't leave Elijah to his thoughts of despair. He didn't chide
him for not believing that He could save him miraculously. After
all, he had just seen an impressive scene the day before, and had
been given supernatural strength to outrun a chariot. Couldn't God
deliver him from the wicked, Baal-serving Queen? Yet, all that we
see is love, compassion, and tenderness from the angel. Oh, this
warmed my heart! It is thought that the "angel of Lord" is actually the Lord Jesus Christ. What a blessing to have Jesus coming
to you, touching you in your fatigue, preparing a meal for you and
beckoning you to come and eat so that you can be strengthened!
How encouraging it must have been to hear Him say, "the journey
is too great for thee." He understands that we can't do this on our
own, and He is there for us, giving us the sustenance that we need
to make the journey and actually get through it.

"And he arose, and did eat and drink, and went
in the strength of that meat forty days and forty
nights unto Horeb the mount of God."

Isn't that amazing?! It made me stop and think, "What is the Lord giving to me right now that is going to give me the strength to make it through this terrible suffering?"

"And he came thither unto a cave, and lodged there; and, behold,
the word of the LORD came to him, and He said unto him,
What doest thou here, Elijah? And he said, I have been very
jealous for the LORD God of hosts: for the children of Israel have
forsaken Thy covenant, thrown down Thine altars, and slain
Thy prophets with the sword; and I, even I only, am left; and
they seek my life, to take it away. And He said, Go forth, and
stand upon the mount before the LORD. And, behold, the LORD
passed by, and a great and strong wind rent the mountains,
and brake in pieces the rocks before the LORD; but the LORD
was not in the wind: and after the wind an earthquake; but
the LORD was not in the earthquake: And after the earthquake
a fire; but the LORD was not in the fire: and after the fire a
still small voice. And it was so, when Elijah heard it, that he
wrapped his face in his mantle, and went out, and stood in the
entering in of the cave. And, behold, there came a voice unto
him, and said, What doest thou here, Elijah? And he said, I
have been very jealous for the LORD God of hosts: because the
children of Israel have forsaken Thy covenant, thrown down
Thine altars, and slain Thy prophets with the sword; and I,
even I only, am left; and they seek my life, to take it away."

—I Kings 19:9-14

I always found it interesting that the Lord was not in the "loud" forces of nature, but He spoke in the still, small voice. Once again, the tenderness and compassion of the Lord comes through in this story. Then the Lord encourages him by instructing him to go back, and on his way, to anoint certain people for specific tasks, one of them being a successor to him, Elisha. He concludes by assuring Elijah that he wasn't the only one left in Israel who served the Lord:

> *"Yet I have left Me seven thousand in Israel, all*
> *the knees which have not bowed unto Baal, and*
> *every mouth which hath not kissed him."*

—I Kings 19:18

This account really showed me how the Lord deals with us when we are brought so low by suffering. Rather than criticizing, reprimanding or completely giving up on us weak creatures, He is "merciful and gracious; slow to anger and plenteous in mercy... He has not dealt with us after our sins; nor rewarded us according to our iniquities. For as the heaven is high above the earth, so great is His mercy toward them that fear Him. As far as the east is from the west, so far hath He removed our transgressions from us. Like as a father pitieth His children, so the Lord pitieth them that fear Him. For He knoweth our frame; He remembereth that we are dust." (Psalm 103:8-14)

I just love that last verse. He knows what we are made of. He knows how weak we are, and instead of judging us and scorning us, He pities us. He comes alongside and helps us, as He did Elijah. He encourages us in our pain and weakness.

It is my prayer and hope that the Lord will surround you with His care and touch your heart with His healing hand so that, today, you will experience the sustenance that He alone can give you. I pray that you may have a little taste of the deep, rich, and full work of healing He will do in your heart.

Chapter 13

God Sees and Cares

*"And God heard their groaning, and God remembered His
covenant with Abraham, with Isaac, and with Jacob.*

*And God looked upon the children of Israel,
and God had respect unto them."*

—Exodus 2:24-25

This Scripture has brought comfort to me over and over again, especially as it relates to the loss of Serena (and our miscarriages). In those initial days, weeks, and months after our loss, God was *there*. He saw our broken hearts. He saw our tears. He saw the pain and the anguish, and He saw the holes in our hearts. However, sometimes it felt like He didn't see; as if He didn't understand or care. Sometimes it felt that He had turned away His face and was not answering.

I am sure the Israelites felt the same way as day after day they slaved away for the Egyptians. Day after day, they were beaten and oppressed, and it seemed like there would be no respite. Day after day, their baby boys were thrown into the Nile River at the Pharaoh's command. But, as one who has walked through this valley and come out through the darkest part of it, I assure you that God *does* see, He hears, and He will bring deliverance. It may not be as soon as we would like it to be, but even the waiting is being used by God to work good in our lives.

As the years have gone by, God continues to remind me that He is there, He hears, He sees, and He remembers. There are times when I find myself grieved or discouraged by the responses of others and as I pour out my heart to Him, it is as if He softly whispers, "But *I* remember, *I* care, *I* see and *I* hear." I then have to ask myself, "Isn't that enough?"

I encourage you, dear mother, when it feels like others don't remember; when it seems that others don't acknowledge that you are still a mother to another child, though that child is not living here on this earth; when year after year, the day goes by, and even those close to you don't acknowledge your precious child's anniversary or reach out to let you know that they are thinking of you and the pain that you carry, remind yourself that **God** remembers. **He** sees. **He** hears those silent groans within. **He** hears your heart's cries to hold that child just one more time, to caress those cheeks one more time, to whisper one more time how much you love that child and desire to hold him/her close to you. And if the Creator of the Universe knows and cares, how honored and privileged are we!

In the months following our little girl's passing into glory, I sang this tender hymn for the first time at my Bible Study. I hadn't ever heard it before, but as I sang, tears flowed down my cheeks. It helped to remind me of the truths that I knew in my head, but was having a hard time believing in the midst of all of the pain and sorrow. To this day, it remains a reminder that brings me comfort when life is challenging. I hope that it will bring you comfort in your sorrow as well.

DOES JESUS CARE?

BY FRANK E. GRAEFF, 1901

Does Jesus care when my heart is pained
Too deeply for mirth or song,
As the burdens press, and the cares distress,
And the way grows weary and long?

Oh, yes, He cares, I know He cares,
His heart is touched with my grief;
When the days are weary, the long nights dreary,
I know my Savior cares.

Does Jesus care when my way is dark
With a nameless dread and fear?
As the daylight fades into deep night shades,
Does He care enough to be near?

Oh, yes, He cares, I know He cares,
His heart is touched with my grief;
When the days are weary, the long nights dreary,
I know my Savior cares.

Does Jesus care when I've tried and failed
To resist some temptation strong;
When for my deep grief there is no relief,
Though my tears flow all the night long?

Oh, yes, He cares, I know He cares,
His heart is touched with my grief;
When the days are weary, the long nights dreary,
I know my Savior cares.

Does Jesus care when I've said "goodbye"
To the dearest on earth to me,
And my sad heart aches till it nearly breaks—
Is it aught to Him? Does He see?

Oh, yes, He cares, I know He cares,
His heart is touched with my grief;
When the days are weary, the long nights dreary,
I know my Savior cares.

"*Ye have lost a child—nay, she is not lost to you, who is found to Christ; she is not sent away, but only sent before; like unto a star, which going out of our sight, doth not die and vanish, but shineth in another hemisphere.*"

—Samuel Rutherford

Chapter 14

When "Failure" Is Actually Success

"It was all a failure!"

"YOU are just a failure!"

Do those words ring in your ears as you think about the death of your precious child? Do the questions haunt you about how you could have done things differently, how if you had just done x, y, and z, the outcome would have been different? You might look at the lifeless body of your child and think that it is all a failure; that *you* are the failure.

I wrestled with feelings of failure after we lost Serena. We had planned a homebirth with a midwife who was highly recommended by friends and relatives. She had thirty years of experience and had delivered over 700 babies. Some people were skeptical about our choice of a homebirth but we assured them that we had a backup plan. We were only ten minutes from the hospital, and would transfer if any signs of distress occurred. Labor started and progressed well, but it was long and hard.

Looking back, there were some things that I could have done differently now that I have had several more full-term labors since then, but this was my first time, and I was relying on my midwife's guidance to know what to do. Our little girl's heartbeat remained strong and steady through contractions and our long labor. We were almost there—my husband saw her head, but I didn't have the strength for the final part of the pushing after the hours of pushing I had already endured. I rested for a while, and it was then that we lost her heartbeat. We made it faster to the hospital than it would have taken for the ambulance to get to our home and transport me. At the hospital, they thought that the heartbeat was still there, but the monitor was picking up my heartbeat and not hers. They did an ultrasound and saw that the chambers of her heart were no longer moving. She was gone.

As reality sunk in during the next hours, days, and weeks, I felt like a failure. First, I had miscarried our very first child at eleven-and-a-half weeks; now, our baby girl was gone. What was I doing wrong? If only I could have had more strength to push… if only I had not gotten so tired and swollen… if only I could have just gotten her out when my husband could see her head (by the way, I did end up delivering naturally, so it wasn't a matter of her being too big). If only… it went on and on as Satan delighted in tormenting me. Feelings of failure loomed over me. Guilt threatened to drown me. I felt like life was no longer worth living. I didn't want to go out in public much because I didn't want to face people who would ask questions about it. I didn't want to see those people who had been skeptical about our choice and were worried that we were doing a homebirth. For the first few months, I just wanted to curl up and hide.

That year, we were studying the Gospel of John in Bible Study Fellowship, and as we went through the chapters around Jesus' death, a whole new light was shed on His sacrifice. To the world, Christ looked like a failure. His death on the cross appeared to be a huge failure. He didn't fulfill the expectations of His followers or the Jewish people who thought He was going to be an earthly king to them; a deliverer from the Roman rule. Just at the moment when it seemed like God's plan had failed, it was the biggest victory in all of history. Jesus said, "It is finished," but the atonement was made! He had to look like a failure in order for the victory to be won.

That single realization caused my whole perspective to change. God could have saved our baby girl, Serena, despite anything "wrong" that I may have done or anything my midwife may have missed. While we have to be wise and use the knowledge that God gives us rather than be foolish and negligent, sometimes things occur completely outside of our power, knowledge, and understanding. God is able to override all of our human weakness and frailty. And so, God could have saved her. He could have even brought her back to life. But He didn't. He had a different plan for her.

I am convinced that what looked like a failure to the hospital, the medical team, my midwife, my husband and I, to family and friends, and many others, was not a failure in God's eyes. It was part of His plan—a very different plan than what we had for our daughter, but it was definitely His plan. He had a specific way that He would use her. It wasn't going to be through a miracle birth or resuscitation. It wasn't going to be through an energetic, vibrant life. It wasn't going to be through living here on earth for His glory. Rather, it was going to be like a seed falling into the ground and dying so that life could be had by others. She gained eternal life in an instant. She had an "express flight" to heaven, as I like to say. He would use her to change me, and to change my husband. He would use her to teach me valuable lessons that I would never have learned if she had lived, and to impact our children and many others that He would bring into our lives. It was not a failure. It was precisely what God had planned.

THREE YEARS AGO

Three years ago, after much hard work and pain,
A beautiful little girl was born
But it seemed it was all in vain.
For some reason unknown to us
She was unable to breathe;
Her days had been fulfilled
It was time for her to leave.
Much sorrow and so many tears
Such heartache and deep grief;
And yet through it all, God brought
His healing hand and incomprehensible relief.
Three years of learning more about Him,
Three years of seeing His loving hand;
Three years of friendships
With those who also can truly understand.
May this day be full of peace
Reflection on the perfect plan of our Father;
Realizing He has brought glory to Himself

And continues to touch people's
lives through your daughter.

So it was far from being in vain

All those tears, hard work and pain;

Through her life and death

There has been **much** gain.

Camilla Neff, August 2012 (penned for
the 3rd anniversary of Sarita Joy Feenstra,
daughter of Mark and Bethany Feenstra)

Chapter 15

Forgiveness

> *"Then said Jesus, 'Father, forgive them;*
> *for they know not what they do.'"*
>
> —Luke 23:34

With Mother's Day having passed a couple weeks ago, and Father's Day approaching in a few weeks, deep emotions frequently resurface, stirring up grief in our hearts. Depending on what our loss looks like, our feelings and emotions could be different, but I am sure that bereaved mothers and fathers all feel a similar aspect of grief on these days. One year, I received an e-mail from a close friend around Mother's Day. The e-mail was not specifically for Mother's Day, but in response to the photo of our children with our newest little one, and while I understand that this friend meant only good by what she wrote, it was painful to read:

"I am so happy to see you a mother of five!"

A deep pain seared through my heart as I read those words (along with some other words that hurt quite a bit as well). Again,

I know she was very well-meaning, but that didn't negate the pain I felt. Inside, my heart screamed, "I am NOT a mother of five, I am a mother of at least six!" No matter how many years pass or how many children I have after losing Serena, her mark is forever in my heart. She is a crucial part of who I am now, and yet it is hard for others to acknowledge this without her physical presence being here.

Perhaps you have received similar comments that bring pain to your heart and "pick" at the scab that has formed over the deep wound of losing your child. It is easy to become bitter, resentful, and unforgiving when you endure the comments of well-meaning, but ignorant, people year after year. In an effort to try to give you some peace, or sometimes just because they don't know what to say, they can say things that add to your burden rather than alleviate it. There have been times when I have wanted to lash back, but that would have done nothing to help the pain subside in my heart. Maybe it will for the moment, but once the tongue-lashing has ceased, there are only more wounds, and perhaps a loss of a relationship.

About four years after we lost Serena, we were asked by a couple of family members to take the photos of Serena off of the walls in our home when they would come for a visit. It has been several years since that request was made, and I cannot remember the exact reasons. I think it had to do with the fact that the photos we have of her are photos of her as dead rather than a photo of a living person that has since died. From what I gather, they considered it a photo of a corpse, and they didn't want their children exposed to such photos. (There may have been other factors surrounding it as well, as other family members had some interesting ideas about how our daughter lacked personhood because she never breathed outside of the womb, along with other interesting thoughts.)

I share this with you just to encourage you that if you have had what feels like cruel, insensitive things said to you, or have been asked to do, or not do, something that hurts deeply, please know you are not alone. While that pain may feel like it is ripping you apart, Jesus can heal that pain too. No pain is too deep for Him to heal.

Initially, I was ready to dig my heels in and resist their request to take down the photos. There was a lot I felt like saying and doing. But, as I mused on the request, I felt like Jesus was asking me to give that "right" up. It was as if He wanted me to show them that I was willing to acquiesce to their request rather than ruin our relationship. It was one more area where He was asking me to sacrifice in order to follow His way. So, we replied that we would take down her photos whenever they came and would put them back up when they left.

I have to confess that those first times of taking down her photos when they were coming over felt I was like ripping off a piece of myself. This was *my* daughter, and if I had photos of her alive, then, by all means, they would be the photos on the wall. Regrettably, the only photos I have of her are photos of her body after she took her flight to Jesus. Regardless of how I felt, I took them down anyway. I will admit that there were times I forgot, and I apologized to them. They were very gracious about it. However, each time I took them down, I think Jesus healed one more aspect of my heart. As I chose to take up my cross and follow Him, rather than stake my cross in the ground and stubbornly refuse to move forward, He brought me deeper into healing. I share this story with you in order that you can see how Jesus can bring healing to your heart and help you forgive when others would think it is impossible, and even unwarranted, to forgive.

I have come to see these painful times as another opportunity for me to learn to be like Christ; to respond with grace and love rather than harboring resentment and bitterness. This is a difficult pill to swallow, and it is very challenging to be like Christ when it strikes at something so near to our heart. Remembering Christ hanging on the cross, bleeding with a crown of thorns on His head, and still being able to say, "Father, forgive them, for they know not what they do" ... *This* is what spurs me on to follow His footsteps.

Remembering His humility on the cross enables me to cry out to Him to help me to forgive, to smile in kindness and love at those who have thrust another dart through my heart, and to run to Him for the healing and balm that I need. It reminds me once again that my only source of true peace and comfort comes from Him. Though I have relationships in my life, none of them can be what only Christ is to be to me: my All in all. If I am looking to others to find the acknowledgment, peace, healing and everything I need to get through the pain of the loss of my child, they will fail me. This is a burden that I cannot place on them. Only Christ can be the true Healer and perfect Comforter for me.

These times of pain are actually reminders that this world is not my home, and they bring my focus back on the One who forgave me for I "do not know what (I) do." If He forgave me for everything I have done to Him, I need to show the love of Christ to those who hurt me, whether intentionally or unintentionally. When weakened by the loss of a child, I think it is doubly hard to forgive, but this is the beauty of our Good Shepherd. He comes alongside us and gives us the grace, even when we don't want to forgive.

A couple of things that help me when I struggle with forgiveness is reminding myself that:

- Unforgiveness will hinder my growth and keep me from moving forward. It keeps me focused on the past.

- Unforgiveness hinders me from growing in my relationship with the Lord. It is a continual distraction.

- Unforgiveness makes me bitter, and ultimately, unforgiveness is disobedience to God.

Someone once said, "We are the most like Jesus when we forgive" and keeping that truth in the forefront of my mind when these painful situations arise helps me to choose what I know is right even when I don't feel like doing it. When we forgive, God is glorified, His power is once again displayed, and we are free. We are *free!*

I encourage you, dear bereaved mother, run to Christ for grace to forgive, and through it all, you will come to know the mind of Christ on a deeper level than you ever thought possible. He will use this pain for your good, transforming you more into His image each and every day.

Chapter 16

Four-Month Birthday

Dear grieving mother,

Four months have passed. Do you wish that you could erase the tragedy and live life as you did before that awful day happened? Are you struggling with knowing how to begin to live life again? Are you wondering if the ache will ever go away? Perhaps you are struggling with certain relationships; they are able to move on with their lives, but you are still figuring out how to simply live another day when those moments of pain begin to sting terribly again. Perhaps you may feel like you should be able to get back to a regular routine by now, and you're left to wonder if you ever will. Please be patient with yourself.

On the other hand, you may find yourself starting to be able to laugh, enjoy time with friends and family, and the tears are flowing less frequently. You might even begin to feel guilty for being able to enjoy life again when these traumatic experiences occurred only a short while ago. Please don't feel guilty. Enjoy those moments of happiness when they come. Continue to learn how to live again without your precious little one. If he or she could speak to you from heaven, they would likely tell you not to grieve and mourn for them—they are enjoying so much perfection, peace, and joy with Jesus. They would want you to rejoice in the hope that we have and in the beauty that Jesus will make out of this. It doesn't mean that you have betrayed them or don't love them. It just means that the millions of shattered pieces of your heart are starting to be glued back together, and the healing process has begun. Thank the Lord for the moments of relief and for the sun peeking through the clouds, for there will likely be more challenging days ahead. The hard days often come and go, sometimes taking us by surprise. However, for now, enjoy the tear-free days, for He does truly heal the broken in heart and bind up their wounds.

Chapter 17

Holidays and Festive Times

The holidays tend to be a busy time with flurries of activities, events to attend, and preparation for the days ahead. Yet, for those of us who have lost our precious children, this time of year can be incredibly painful. We may not even want to face this season when our heart is aching so badly. While everyone is celebrating with cheer and joy, it takes tremendous effort to simply wear a smile, much less look forward to the New Year with happiness. As if that wasn't hard enough on its own, people often forget about our loss as they are caught up in the busyness, and we are left feeling forgotten and alone in our pain.

Take heart, dear mother.

Jesus knows.

He hasn't forgotten. He hasn't become so preoccupied with the flurry of activities or the problems of others that He has no time for you. *Every* moment that you need from Him, He has available for you. He knows all of the dreams that you had for your precious one. He knows all of the hopes and plans that you had. He knows the ache in your heart that you can't describe in words. He knows every emotion that you are experiencing right now. And He comes beside you and lifts you up. When you are too tired to walk on your own, He carries you. When you can barely get a smile out, He can give you one. When you just want to curl up and hide, His arms are open wide, ready to embrace you with the depth of love that no one else in this world can offer to you. Come to Jesus. Pour out your heart to Him. Share all of your pain, your emotions, your questions, and your doubts. He understands. He desires to be your refuge, your comfort, and your balm.

When I am feeling the pain and the absence of our little girl, Serena Nadine; when my heart can't take the lonely ache any more, or when I look at our family photo and "see" that empty place where she would have been, right alongside the rest of our little blessings, it helps me to remember that it is because of Christ's coming, His love, and His sacrifice that her death was not the end, but just the beginning. There is no doubt that it felt like the end, but in reality, it was just the beginning—it was the beginning of an eternity of peace, rest, and security in Christ. Had He never come, became man and dwelt among us; had He never endured the pain and suffering of the cross so that we could be bought back from the fall, she would never know the peace and joy that she now has for eternity.

This gives me hope to move on, to continue to smile through the tears, knowing that Jesus loved my little girl so much that He died for her that she could live. This brings me peace in the midst of the pain, the loneliness of grief, and the aching heart, and it is my hope that it will do the same for you.

Chapter 18

The New Year

A new year has begun. For some, there are New Year's resolutions. For others, they are looking forward to a new start—better things, or a more prosperous life. For those of us who have lost our children, it may be very different. Our whole perspective on life has changed. Some of us might be looking forward to a new year, hoping to be able to put behind us the year that was full of devastation. For others, we are just not ready to start a new year. Time may have stopped for you as it did for me. I vividly remember one Sunday morning in October when my husband and I were driving to church, and it dawned on me that the leaves had all changed color and were dropping to the ground. "Really?" I wondered aloud. "How is it already October?!"

When we lost Baby Gad to a miscarriage at eleven-and-a-half weeks, a friend of mine who had lost her son at birth several years before encouraged me not to put a timeline on grief. "Don't expect to be over it by December," she had counseled me, and that thought continued with me when we lost Serena.

I am so thankful the Lord doesn't expect us to be over our loss within a specific timeframe. He is a loving Shepherd, gently leading His beloved sheep through each and every trial that they go through. As the time passes, we will find that the ache lessens, the sharp sting diminishes, and the rawness of our shredded heart isn't as sensitive, but I do believe bereaved parents never truly "get over" the loss of a child. There are the yearly anniversaries, the would-be birthdays, the family photos where that child would be present, the children in other families that were born around the same time frame as our deceased child and they are now growing up, maturing, and doing all sorts of things that we envision our child would have been doing. There are the quiet moments, the strangest phrases or situations that trigger the memories we have of our little ones. I believe all of that is a part of the special bond that we have with our child who is no longer with us. Though others' lives move on, and it often seems that they have forgotten that we have an unseen member of our family, our little one's life is etched on our heart, never to be forgotten.

With this New Year beginning, I would encourage you, dear mother, to reflect on how this devastating trial can be used in your life for the glory of God and the good of others. You might not be ready yet to step out and do anything because your heart is still so broken. From my experience, I have seen that taking the opportunities that the Lord provided me with and stepping out in faith, trusting Him to bless it, helped me along in the healing process. By reaching out to others, it took the focus off of me and my pain and helped me use what God had entrusted to me to demonstrate His grace and loving kindness to those around me. It was not easy. It was much easier to sit back and remain in my comfort zone, building a wall around myself as I dealt with the pain in my heart. But, it seemed that the Lord was asking me to reach out to others when it would have been much easier to shut myself off. Yes, He was calling me to continue to face my pain, cry when I needed and soothe my soul with His promises and Word, but to also look beyond my circumstances and help others in the trials that they were facing.

I want to encourage you as well to look for the opportunities that God is bringing into your life to help you step out of your comfort zone and heal through ministering to others. For me, there were opportunities to babysit my little nephew, who was just a month older than what Serena was. He stayed overnight while his parents went away for a couple of days, and I found that it was mixed with pain and blessing. But, the Lord used that to help heal me. There were times where I didn't want to see anyone but chose to reach out and connect with others, learning about the challenges that they were facing and seeing how I could help them, rather than merely focusing on my own pain.

There were also times where I didn't want to talk to family members because it hurt so badly not to have anything else to talk about in my life besides the intense grief I was going through. No one had experienced the same pain, so they really didn't know what to say. It hurt not to hear my little brother ask me how the baby was doing anymore because the baby was now dead. Before she died, at the end of his conversation, he would always say, "Tell the baby that I love it too," and it would make me smile. Now, there was nothing asked about the baby, and the silence just stirred the anguish in my heart. It wasn't his fault, of course. But choosing to still call and talk about what was going on in his life was something I found I needed to do.

Praying for other expectant mothers to have healthy pregnancies and safe deliveries was another practical thing that the Lord was calling me to do.

The Lord may be calling you to do some of the same things, or He may be calling you to different ways of glorifying Him through your suffering. Ask Him to open your eyes so that you can see the opportunities that He is bringing your way, for in answering His call of service, despite your pain, you will find that healing is sure to come.

*"Blessed be God, even the Father of our Lord Jesus Christ,
the Father of mercies, and the God of all comfort; Who
comforteth us in all our tribulation, that we may be
able to comfort them which are in any trouble, by the
comfort wherewith we ourselves are comforted of God."*

—II Corinthians 1:3-4

Chapter 19

Being Faithful with What the Lord Has Given

In the last chapter, I encouraged you to reach out and embrace the opportunities the Lord brings into our lives to help or serve others, even as we are walking through our own journey with pain. Some of us may be wondering how we can move on, feeling like we have nothing to contribute to those around us because of the deep sorrow. We are wondering how we can "pick up the pieces" and live a fruit-filled life.

I have found that at my darkest moments, the Lord brings passages of Scripture to minister to my heart and show me the purpose and plan that He has for my life. Below is a parable that Jesus spoke to His listeners:

"For the kingdom of heaven is as a man travelling into a far country, who called his own servants, and delivered unto them his goods. And unto one he gave five talents, to another two, and to another one; to every man according to his several ability; and straightway took his journey. Then he that had received the five talents went and traded with the same, and made them other five talents. And likewise he that had received two, he also gained other two. But he that had received one went and digged in the earth, and hid his lord's money. After a long time the lord of those servants cometh, and reckoneth with them. And so he that had received five talents came and brought other five talents, saying, Lord, thou deliveredst unto me five talents: behold, I have gained beside them five talents more. His lord said unto him, Well done, thou good and faithful servant: thou hast been faithful over a few things, I will make thee ruler over many things: enter thou into the joy of thy lord. He also that had received two talents came and said, Lord, thou deliveredst unto me two talents: behold, I have gained two other talents beside them. His lord said unto him, Well done, good and faithful servant; thou hast been faithful over a few things, I will make thee ruler over many things: enter thou into the joy of thy lord. Then he which had received the one talent came and said, Lord, I knew thee that thou art an hard man, reaping where thou hast not sown, and gathering where thou hast not strawed: And I was afraid, and went and hid thy talent in the earth: lo, there thou hast that is thine. His lord answered and said unto him, Thou wicked and slothful servant, thou knewest that I reap where I sowed not, and gather where I have not strawed: Thou oughtest therefore to have put my money to the exchangers, and then at my coming I should have received mine own

with usury. Take therefore the talent from him, and give it unto him which hath ten talents. For unto every one that hath shall be given, and he shall have abundance: but from him that hath not shall be taken away even that which he hath. And cast ye the unprofitable servant into outer darkness: there shall be weeping and gnashing of teeth."

—Matthew 25:14-30

There are a few "nuggets" that have helped me tremendously over the years; I hope they will be a blessing to you as well.

1. **God doesn't deal with everyone in a "cookie cutter" fashion.**

   I have mentioned this before, but this was one of those lessons that He kept bringing back to mind over and over as I experienced losses when those around me were experiencing outward blessing. The master gave five talents to one servant, two talents to another, and one talent to another. To each, it was something different, but He expected them all to use what He had given faithfully.

2. **The first two servants used what they were given.**

   The one who received two talents didn't complain because he wasn't given five, and the one with five didn't gloat in the fact that he received five while the other servants received less. Each of them focused on what they had been given and worked with what was entrusted to their care.

3. **The master was pleased with the diligent servants.**

   He didn't expect more of the one that was given less. He was pleased with what each had accomplished. What He noted was their *faithfulness*. He encouraged them both and promised them further responsibilities. He welcomed them into "the joy of your lord."

4. **The 3rd servant was afraid and misjudged his master.**

   This induced him to do nothing with what he was given, but instead, he hid his talent in the ground.

5. **The master was not pleased with the 3rd servant.**

   He called him a "wicked and slothful servant." He also called him an "unprofitable servant" and condemned him to outer darkness. He also took the talent from him and gave it to one of the servants that had been faithful.

This parable has encouraged me to focus on the fact that what concerns the Lord most is that we are **faithful** with what He gives to us. He doesn't give us all the same blessings, the same challenges, or the same trials, but what He does give to us, He gives to us in love and desires that we use it for His glory and the good of others. I have found that focusing on what He did give to me rather than on what He had given to others helped me to see the beauty in the opportunities He had placed before me. When I switched my perspective to look at the "talents" He had given me, I began to see the unique ways He was calling me to shine forth His love, power, goodness, peace, joy and His incredible grace. These characteristics of Jesus reach far beyond the pain that we experience in this life and transform us into beautiful vessels that bear the imprint of His craftsmanship as He orchestrates every situation and circumstance in our lives.

At times, we may feel like we are just "broken vessels of clay," fit for nothing but the garbage heap. There were times where I felt so broken that I asked the Lord to take me home. The pain was so great that I felt like I was failing every one of the tests that He had given to me. My faith faltered often; I often succumbed to doubt and fear. Anger overwhelmed me, and I felt like there was no reason for Him to keep me living on this earth, for I didn't consider myself a shining light for His kingdom.

But it was in that very brokenness that He was blessing me. He was showing me my utter dependence on Him. He was revealing all of the wickedness that my natural heart was inclined toward without the presence of His Spirit, breaking my pride, and humbling me so that I could be a tool in His hand to bring about encouragement and blessing to others. Through the anguish and pain, He taught me compassion and gave me an understanding of others. He gave me a deeper sense of love for the hurting. He made it clear that things that were once a "big deal" really weren't a big deal at all in the grand scheme of things. He taught me that I am not in control of my life or others' lives, and I had to learn to let go. In essence, He revealed to me more of the way that He views things and instilled in my heart more of His character.

So, when you are tempted to feel hopeless, useless and unsure of how all the "broken pieces of pottery" in your life could ever become a beautiful masterpiece, I pray that He will grant you eyes to see the special opportunities that He will bring into your life this year. I pray that you would be able to see a glimpse of how He will use all of those broken pieces to bless you and others as you are faithful to use this trial in your life for His glory.

Chapter 20

Five-Month Birthday

Dear grieving mother,

Another month has passed. I remember visiting my family in Canada over the holidays when Serena's 5th month birthday was approaching. At one of our extended family dinners, my cousin's wife came up to me.

"You know, I had a dream that you were pregnant," she said.

I admit I wondered where this was going, as my extended family has a "talent" for having dreams about pregnancy if they think there is even the slightest chance you are expecting.

She continued, "In the dream, I asked you, 'Are you going to have it in the hospital?' And you said, 'Yes.'"

I knew what she was getting at, and it was like salt being poured into my wounds. That was my first visit back to my "homeland" since I lost Serena, and I felt the silent criticism and condemnation for our choice of birth location and the subsequent outcome.

I had had a text conversation with another cousin who had labeled the situation the "assassination of Serena." Heart-stabbing, to say the least!

Just a month earlier, on the day after I miscarried our 3rd baby, another close family member gave me their thoughts about the whole scenario over chat. I remember sitting at the table, staring blankly at my computer screen with tears coursing down my cheeks. I can't even begin to describe the excruciating pain that seared through my being. Another family member said that my body "aborted" all three of my pregnancies—that my body "rejected" Serena, and they had an idea of the reason why, but didn't disclose it. Writhing in pain may be a description that somewhat conveys the depth of what I was experiencing from the insensitive comments spoken.

Perhaps you have experienced the same thing. Maybe there are friends or family who feel that the initial, terrible pain is over for you now, and as they are trying to cope with the loss, they begin to share their thoughts of how it all went wrong, how it could have been prevented, etc. I am sure that they do not understand how heart wrenching this is for you. They likely haven't sat down to consider just what their comments are implying. Perhaps they don't realize that if you could have changed anything to bring your precious little one back, you definitely would have. Little do they understand that talking about the "what ifs" and "should haves" really are not going to help you stop reeling from the pain and learn to live a new normal.

If this has happened to you, I am so sorry. I pray that the Lord will apply His soothing balm to your heart once again. I pray that His arms would hold you tight as you fall into them, weary and fatigued, exhausted with the pain and drained of all emotion and energy to lovingly respond to those who are well-intentioned but insensitive. I pray that He will give you a heart full of love to respond to those who simply do not (and **cannot**) understand in the way that Jesus did, saying from the cross, "Father, forgive them, for they know not what they do."

Chapter 21

Nuggets on Suffering

> *"Measure thy life by loss instead of gain;*
> *Not by the wine drunk, but the wine poured forth;*
> *For love's strength standeth in love's sacrifice;*
> *And whoso suffers most hath most to give…"*

—Ugo Bassi

As I sit down to write, my mind drifts back to this date seven years ago- the date our very first little one was due. That sweet baby, Baby Gad, was granted to us for eleven-and-a-half weeks in the womb and then went to be with our Savior. It was quite the blow for us emotionally, and though I never got to meet that little one outside the womb, he or she has (and will always have) a special place in my heart. The Lord used his or her short life and subsequent death to teach me lessons I never even knew I needed to learn.

Seven years later, on this day, I am due with our 6th full term child. I would love for this baby to come today, turning a day that was *supposed to be* full of joy and happiness into a day of *true* joy and happiness. Who knows what God's plans are for this child and its arrival?

As I went through the labor to deliver our very first baby, I remember lying on the bed, crying out in frustration, bewilderment, and anger to God. I couldn't understand why He was allowing this to happen to us. It was incredibly difficult to see how this could possibly be worked out for good in our lives. I was ready to suffer *big* things for God, like persecution for believing in Him, rejection from the world for following Him, being sneered at for my standards that were based on Scripture... but to lose my child? That wasn't exactly my picture of what suffering for Christ would look like.

I expected that because we had followed His commands and had a desire to build a family for His glory that He would bless our obedience. I expected that He would grant life to the children we conceived because we had His glory as our chief purpose and aim. This kind of suffering was not what I imagined when I thought of the gems He would fit in the crown of life that He is preparing for me.

Little did I know then that the death of this little one at eleven-and-a-half weeks in the womb was preparing me for a harder blow I would experience ten months later when Serena would die during labor. The lessons that God was teaching me from *this* miscarriage would be further dug into, searing into my entire being through Serena's death. Little did I know how He would use that suffering for purposes far beyond what I would ever imagine or comprehend.

We don't get to choose the unique suffering that we will endure in our lives. Thankfully, God knows exactly what we need, even when it doesn't make sense to us. As a loving Father, God brings tailor-made trials in our life in order to make us more like Him, to impact others' lives, and to fashion us into the beautiful masterpiece He has created us to be before the foundations of the earth were formed. He is making us joint-heirs in glory with Christ as we suffer with Him. And isn't that a privilege?

Over the years, the Lord has greatly ministered to my heart through the notes from Bible Study Fellowship. One lesson was particularly rich with encouragement as it addressed suffering and God's plan through those painful experiences. It brought incredible refreshment to my soul every time I've read them, and I wanted to share a synopsis of the Notes in hopes that they can be encouraging to you as well as you navigate the journey of loss.

1. **God strategically places difficult circumstances in our lives for good purposes.**

   In the example of Daniel's captivity, God did not merely make the best of this circumstance, but instead, He strategically placed Daniel in Babylon to fulfill the purposes that He had planned. You may feel that this is only applicable to extraordinary people and in special situations, but please be encouraged: this is true for every person who loves and trusts in the Lord Jesus Christ. God has strategically placed you in unique circumstances that He will use to fulfill His purposes. No matter where God places His people, He *will* accomplish His perfect will through them. We can ask ourselves, "Where has God placed me? For what purpose has He allowed me to go through this pain?"

2. **God has good purposes in every single situation and circumstance that He allows in our lives.**

   The people of God will suffer, and that suffering may be terribly painful. Sometimes we think that because we have been promised abundant life in Christ, we will live a life free of pain and suffering, that everything will go just as we want, and that the blessings God promises will be only good things. When we are tempted to think that the path of blessing refers to God's pleasure and that suffering in our life is not congruent with that path, we must remember that the Bible teaches otherwise. We can gain courage from the truth that the abundant life in Christ is a result of a life wherein God is glorified as we find our strength and joy in Him, even in the midst of suffering. When we remember that God loves us so much that He cannot spare us from the integral character development and refinement that comes only through pain, our perspective on suffering will change.

This is an extremely difficult truth to swallow, to say the least. However, it may be easier to accept if you look back over your walk with Jesus. When did you see the greatest times of growth in your life? Was it not when you were going through times that were uncomfortable, painful and challenging? If your faith was never tested, how would you know the strength of it? When we walk through the valleys, the truth about our faith is revealed. God lovingly weaves the exact number of struggles we need into our lives we need to keep our reliance and focus on Him. Pain and suffering teach us much about ourselves and our great God.

When we experience the storms and droughts in our life, just as a tree does, we will find our roots are forced further down into our foundation—the Lord Himself. We discover the places that we need to grow, and we are also faced with a choice: will we allow this suffering to harden our hearts, or will we allow it to soften us so that we can hear from and respond to the Lord? Because of the truth that suffering can cause our spiritual life to flourish, let us ever be watchful that the pain is not wasted. Let us look for the opportunities that God will give us to experience abundant life in Christ despite the struggles and remember: God is able to use everything in life, good or bad, to make His children more like Himself. This should bring us deep comfort in the storms of life.

3. **Our heavenly Father loves us too much to let us wallow in our sin.**

He lovingly allows challenges to come into our lives that we may be refined and grow in our Christ-likeness. When we undergo this discipline, we can be assured that God loves us deeply. I encourage you to *embrace* the opportunities that God gives you through suffering to grow in faith and Christ-likeness.

4. **Suffering draws us closer to the Lord, despite the reason for it.**

In our finite minds, we are unable to accurately assess why God has allowed the pain we are undergoing, but one thing is certain—we can always pray, learn and grow from it. One question we often battle when walking through suffering is, "Is this God's discipline or is this warfare with Satan? Is this suffering because I have done something terribly wrong, or is it just a part of the natural consequences of a fallen world?" While we may not be able to accurately answer these questions, our suffering can always be used to draw us closer to the Lord. No matter the reason for our suffering, we ought to always search our hearts, asking the

Lord to show us what needs to be changed in our lives, what sin needs to be confessed and what lessons He wants us to learn from our pain. We cannot know God's specific purpose for each hurt we experience, but we do know that God uses every trial, offense, and pain to sanctify His children. Ultimately, the most important thing is to grow through the pain rather than analyzing and categorizing it. Can we be content if we never know the reason for the suffering that God has allowed? This is a very sobering question, but one that helps us along the journey of knowing the peace that passes all understanding.

5. **Suffering tests what we believe.**

Suffering has a way of applying what we believe to the daily struggles that we face. We may feel as if our theology is unshakeable, but when the storms hit, we find our boat is being tossed upon the waves. We may be struggling with understanding why an omniscient, omnipotent and loving God didn't step in and prevent the pain that we are experiencing. Oftentimes these questions (that are honest and legitimate) cannot be answered entirely with our limited minds. We want immediate answers to our questions, but we have to remember that God sees the bigger picture. He is always doing more than what we actually think. We can find comfort in the fact that our inability to completely comprehend God's purposes causes us to find the comfort and stability we are searching for in that which we do know with certainty—God's sovereignty, power, goodness, holiness, and love.

6. **Focus on the unchanging character of our great God.**

Remembering that God is sovereign points us to the fact that He is completely in control of everything at all times. He has the power to effect good out of pain and suffering. He not only *allows* the suffering, but He also *uses it* to mold and shape our faith and character in ways that we would otherwise never know. It may not feel comforting to know that terrible things happen within the scope of God's holy and sovereign control, but wouldn't it be worse to think that evil is more powerful than the Lord? That bad things could randomly happen because God is not in control of them, and to think that nothing good could come out of our experiences with pain? When we are tempted to focus on the devastation causing chaos in our lives, could we actually turn our focus to the Lord and focus on who He is to give us comfort?

7. **God doesn't call believers to equal suffering.**

It is very tempting to compare our lot with others, but we cannot measure our pain against the suffering of family members, friends, fellow church members, etc. Christ calls everyone to deny themselves, yet suffering is going to look different in each believer's life. Jesus spoke to this when Peter questioned what type of suffering John would experience. Jesus had just told Peter that he would experience persecution, and like all of us, Peter wanted to know what John would undergo. Jesus was very clear in His answer to Peter: he didn't need to worry about John; his only responsibility was to follow Christ and the path that He set out for him. And so it should be for us. When we start comparing our suffering with others, it is easy to get trapped in the downward spiral of self-pity, jealousy, envy, and discontentment. But when we focus on the fact that this is what God has specifically called us to, and that He has strategically allowed this particular suffering in our lives and will use it for a specific purpose, we can start to know the depth of His peace and trust His goodness.

8. **God always knows about our pain, and He truly does care.**

Nothing escapes His all-knowing eye and tender heart. When we suffer, we do so knowing that Jesus also experienced real suffering. He can identify with our pain. He experienced physical pain, hunger, and deprivation. He knows the heartbreak of betrayal. He understands the anguish of loss as He wept when Lazarus died, even though He knew He would raise Him from the dead. He identified with us so that we could identify with Him and be co-heirs of the kingdom of God. Will the knowledge that Jesus suffered so that you could be eternally free from pain help you as you walk this path of suffering?

9. **Suffering gives us a greater awareness of the work of the Lord in our lives.**

The little things become opportunities to see how God provides and protects us. We also experience firsthand how He hears and answers those who trust in Him when we cry out to Him fervently in challenging times.

10. **Suffering helps us to know, without a shadow of a doubt, that God is enough.**

He is everything we need. There are times when the only thing God is asking us is to trust Him *in* the pain and *with* the pain. He promises that He will never give us more than we are able to endure. Oftentimes, we think that we cannot endure it, but as He equips us day after day to bear the burden, clinging to Him, we find a strength that we never knew existed.

11. **Suffering invites us to be transformed into the image of Christ.**

As mentioned before, God has good purposes in everything that we undergo, even the most painful of trials. There are times when He works supernaturally and brings protection and relief. Other times, He doesn't. But that doesn't mean that He doesn't have a particular purpose in that suffering. On the contrary, His strength "delivers us through the suffering," causing us to look more and more like our Savior who suffered for us.

There were also some practical questions the Notes urged us to consider:

1. What pain and suffering are you facing? Are you able to rest in God's sovereignty and His goodness? Be open and honest with the Lord, asking Him for faith and perseverance in this trial. As your Father, He loves you, knows you and promises to answer. Reach out in faith to Him and trust Him, even when you cannot understand His purposes.

2. Are you resenting the trials that you are facing right now? After coming before Him in prayer, and asking Him your questions, will you wait with expectation for His answer?

3. Are you willing to allow God to draw you closer to Himself? As your faith is stretched, will you fervently pray and trust the bigger purposes God has planned that you cannot see?

4. Are you willing to move beyond just barely making it through your pain to actually exulting in God's purposes

even if you don't fully understand His plan? Oftentimes, God is doing something far greater than we could ever imagine and it takes more time than we want to wait. In that time of waiting, will you cling to your Father and drink out of the wellsprings of life and strength that He offers to you?

I hope you were not overwhelmed with all of the content I included here. These "nuggets" just encouraged me so much to renew my thinking about suffering and grief. When I focused on the fact that God is sovereign, and not only sovereign but also loving and good, it helped to assuage my fears. This devastation was not in vain. He had the power to take a horrible situation and use it for something good. I pray that these "nuggets" will minister to your heart as they did mine and transform your mind so you can experience a peace that you never thought was possible!

"Think of your child then, not as dead, but as living; not as a flower that has withered, but as one that is transplanted, and touched by a Divine hand, is blooming in richer colors and sweeter shades than those of earth."

—Richard Hooker,
British theologian

Chapter 22

Their Purpose Was (and is Being) Fulfilled

Has this week been one of struggle and intense pain, dear sorrowing one? Has another anniversary passed which brought back fresh memories of the loss of your precious child? Have you had a painful conversation with someone that has ripped off the scab that had begun to cover the wound in your heart, and you feel as if you are once again bleeding in pain and agony? Are you ready to give up?

Dear one, I want to encourage you to take a moment and reflect on something that gives me hope whenever the sting of pain returns: **God has a purpose for each and every one of us, and when that purpose has been fulfilled, He takes us home.**

We all expect to live a long life. We expect that our children will outlive us. We expect that as long as we have done what He commands us to do, our lives will continue on as planned. We expect that we will, at some time, die peacefully and go to heaven. However, we don't expect to stand at the cemetery and watch the casket with our child's body in it be lowered into the ground. We don't expect to have to pick out our children's gravestones. We don't expect to have conversations about how many children we actually have since the number on earth doesn't match the one we have written in our hearts. We don't expect to try to pick up the broken pieces of our hearts when our children have gone before us.

Somehow, we mistakenly think that if someone dies before the time that we had expected, their purpose in life was not fulfilled. We feel that they were cut off before their time. But in the Lord's perspective, it is much different. The little baby He took to be with Himself in the first trimester—whether five weeks or twelve weeks—had a special purpose. Even though they did not live outside of the womb, their purpose was fulfilled. The little baby that He took to be with Himself in the second trimester had a special purpose, and that purpose was fulfilled. The little baby who was full-term, strong and healthy through labor and delivery, then suddenly, for no apparent reason, did not live... even he or she had an extraordinary purpose, and that purpose was fulfilled. The six-month-old, the nine-month-old, the toddler, the preschool or elementary school-aged child... every single individual has a purpose in this life, and when that purpose is fulfilled, God calls them home.

Even still, we can often struggle with the guilt of the "If only's." In our case, it looked like this:

"If only I went to the hospital sooner."

"If only I didn't push so hard."

"If only I knew what that 'urge to push' really felt like."

"If only we had chosen a different midwife."

We can struggle with the "why's":

"Why didn't she tell us…?"

"Why did this have to be God's plan?"

"Why were we chosen to be in this 'club'?"

"Why didn't God answer our prayer the way we were asking?"

We can struggle with the "should have's":

"We should have gone to the hospital sooner."

"We should have listened to a few of the question marks in our mind that we had but dismissed."

"We should have…"

Everyone's situation is different, and I am sure you can identify with the above statements. Whatever your case may be, this truth remains the same: the only place that we can truly find peace from all the questions is in the acknowledgment and trust in God's perfect plan. Knowing that our precious child had a purpose and that they fulfilled that purpose can give us peace and a sense of joy that we otherwise could not have.

My dear friend, in the midst of your struggle and pain, perhaps you can take a moment to reflect on the purpose that your precious child had. Perhaps it was that you might see your need for Christ. Perhaps it was that you might see sins, attitudes, and idols of your heart that God wanted to reveal. Perhaps it was to bring you into closer fellowship with Him. Perhaps it was to show you that life can be gone in a moment's time and that death is not something that will happen sometime out there in the future. Perhaps it was to help you prepare for the return of Christ. Perhaps it was to help you reflect on your priorities in life and focus on the relationships and the lives that you daily interact with. Perhaps it was to minister to others who are watching you walk through loss, and as you cling to Christ, you are a testimony of His grace, power, strength, and peace.

Or, perhaps you don't see the purpose quite yet. Perhaps you're still wrestling with seeing any good that could come out of the intense pain or only see in part. Wherever you may find yourself, be encouraged that whatever it might be, your child had a purpose. There *is* a purpose in what you are going through. Not only that, but they will *continue* to fulfill that purpose as their story and life encourages and comforts others who tread the same path.

Chapter 23

Choose to Love and Have Joy Again

"How can I ever be happy about another pregnancy?"

I remember asking this question of a mature-in-the-faith Christian woman I knew after we lost Serena. Does this same question ring in your ears after the loss of your child during pregnancy, birth or thereafter?

In our story, we lost three babies before experiencing the inexpressible joy of having a living child. While reeling in pain because of the losses, I didn't know how I could ever be happy about future pregnancies. I cannot recall her exact words, but that which was indelibly imprinted on my heart, through the six pregnancies that I have been blessed with since then, has been this:

> "Would you want this new life within not to feel the same love and joy that you had for the one that you lost? Would you want this new life to suffer, feeling rejected or unloved or unwanted, simply because you are trying to guard your heart against further pain?"

The true meaning of love was clearly illuminated: by being vulnerable, opening up my heart to once again love another new little blessing that God had granted, and not holding back for fear of this child being taken from me, I was coming to know the blessedness of putting another's good and benefit before my own. And, if that child were taken by the Lord as well, I would have peace knowing that they knew just how much I loved him or her. These thoughts made the decision very clear for me—I would love each new child with the same unshakable love I had for each of the ones I lost. I would do everything I could to bond with them and regard each one with the same tenderness, care, fondness and joy that I had for my other three pregnancies. If another child were destined for heaven instead of this earth, I wouldn't want that child to die within my womb, feeling my fear to love, my lack of love or unwillingness to bond with him/her merely because I was trying to protect my heart from further pain.

Don't get me wrong; this doesn't mean I didn't struggle with fear, worry, anxiety, and concern during each of my pregnancies. On the contrary, it was a daily struggle, especially with our first living child after our losses. Every day of that pregnancy, I had to "lay him on the altar," just as God asked Abraham to do with Isaac. I had to daily commit him to the Lord, trusting that even if God, in His infinite wisdom, were to take him as well, He had a perfect plan in it all. There were many tears and many fervent prayers consisting of me laying bare my heart before the Lord and His revealing the sinfulness and corruption within me. He illuminated my heart to see the best that He had intended for me and patiently brought me along on that difficult path, teaching me how to trust Him.

So, all that to say, if you find yourself struggling to love again after loss, I encourage you to take the chance and lay your heart on the line. Love deeply and strongly, and don't hold back. Let that next child know that you love him or her just as much as you did your other little one, and you will see God do wonderful things. You will see how God can enable that sacrifice of your fears, tears and emotions to blossom into something that is beautiful, far beyond your imagination.

DEAR LITTLE BABY
(WRITTEN FEBRUARY 26, 2010)

Dear little baby
Growing in my womb,
I'm thinking about you
And fears threaten to loom.
Mommy's tummy is not well
It's hard for me to eat,
And even to drink makes me feel sick
But I want your heart to beat.
You're Mama's little child
The fourth one conceived;
Will you live outside the womb and
Will my arms you receive?
Darling child,
You're in God's hands;
I must not fret and worry

By faith I must stand.
It now has become a choice
Will I worry or will I trust?
I have absolutely no control
And rely on God I must.
So dear little child,
Mama loves you so much;
I want to hold you alive
And kiss your cheeks with fervor such.
But even if God takes you away,
Yes, the tears will flow;
And once again, I'll bless God's name,
Who never let you pain know.
I've come to see the blessed truth
That heaven is a better place.
And even though I'll miss you much
It's better—you'll see Christ's face.
For now, I am God's simple vessel
To house your little life;
We'll see what the ultimate plan is,
I hope He gives you life.

*"Could I refuse Him my child because
she was the very apple of my eye?*

*Nay then, but let me give to Him not what I value least,
but what I prize and delight in most.*

*Could I not endure heartsickness for Him
who had given His only Son for me?"*

—Mrs. Elizabeth Prentiss,
Stepping Heavenward,
June 2 entry; p.313

Chapter 24

Six-Month Birthday

Dear grieving mother,

Six months can be a really tough time. It marks half a year—half a year of pain and sorrow, and only another half a year before you will be facing the first birthday/anniversary of their death. You might be envisioning what it would have been like if your little one was here on earth. They would likely be sitting up, starting on some pureed foods, and maybe sporting a couple of teeth. They would be interacting more with both you and other family members.

You envision your parents playing with them, their giggle at Grandpa's whiskers tickling their cheeks, their full-out grin when their uncles toss them into the air... and then you snap back to reality and see the missing "spot" in the family photos once again. You may feel robbed. Cheated. You may feel that something was "dangled" in front of your face and then whisked away as soon as you reached for it. You may be wishing that it was never dangled in front of your face in the first place because the pain of almost knowing the desire fulfilled is even more devastating.

I just want to encourage you today to "lay your child on the altar." Long ago, God asked Abraham to offer his only son, Isaac—who had been born when he was at the ripe old age of 100 years—on an altar in sacrifice to Him. Without delay, the next morning, Abraham arose and prepared to do exactly what God had asked him to do. I cannot imagine the thoughts that went through his mind, but we get a glimpse into his heart when he answers Isaac's questioning: "God will provide Himself a lamb for the offering." In Hebrews, it says that he trusted God could even raise Isaac from the dead, as he was convinced that God would be true to His promises.

God was faithful and did provide a lamb in place of Isaac. It was right at the last moment, just as Abraham had Isaac bound on the altar and had his arm raised with the knife to slay him. The angel of the Lord called to him and told him not to harm the boy; that he knew that Abraham loved the Lord so much that he was willing not to withhold his son—his only son whom he loved so dearly—from God.

I'll confess that when I first was processing this scripture after our losses, I thought to myself, "Well, at least Abraham got his son back and didn't actually have to give him up to death. My daughter is dead, and she's not coming back to me here on earth." But even though Abraham didn't have to give up his son to death in the end, he had been willing to do so, knowing that God would be true to His promises. As I pondered that lesson over time, I asked myself, *Is my heart as willing to give up my daughter to the Lord as Abraham was?* If I were in Abraham's shoes, would I be able to do whatever God asked of me, even as far as sacrificing my only son, the son of the promise, to the Lord?

When I was pregnant with Caleb, our first living child after Serena, I remember having to lay him on the altar every morning. It meant being willing to give him up to the Lord if He desired to take him home as well. It meant giving up my hopes, desires, and dreams for this child and being a willing vessel to nurture this baby for as long as the Lord granted him life. It was a tearful surrender, and I did it oh so falteringly. This lesson of complete submission is no easy lesson to learn, but surrendering our will to His is the only way that we can find true peace. Accepting His will—bending our will to His—brings a peace that cannot be achieved any other way.

IN ACCEPTANCE LIETH PEACE

BY AMY CARMICHAEL

He said, 'I will forget the dying faces;

The empty places,

They shall be filled again.

O voices moaning deep within me, cease.'

But vain the word; vain, vain:

Not in forgetting lieth peace.

He said, 'I will crowd action upon action,

The strife of faction

Shall stir me and sustain;

O tears that drown the fire of manhood cease.'

But vain the word; vain, vain:

Not in endeavour lieth peace.

He said, 'I will withdraw me and be quiet,

Why meddle in life's riot?

Shut be my door to pain.

Desire, thou dost befool me, thou shalt cease.'

But vain the word; vain, vain:

Not in aloofness lieth peace.

He said, 'I will submit; I am defeated.

God hath depleted

My life of its rich gain.

O futile murmurings, why will ye not cease?'

But vain the word; vain, vain:

Not in submission lieth peace.

He said, 'I will accept the breaking sorrow

Which God tomorrow

Will to His son explain.'

Then did the turmoil deep within me cease.

Not vain the word, not vain;

For in Acceptance lieth peace.

Chapter 25

Battling the Fear Of "What Will God Do Next?"

Are you tormented by the terrifying thought of what God might take away or ask you to do? Maybe you've found yourself thinking, "Will He take my spouse from me next? Will we lose our job? Our home? Our other children? Our parents? Siblings? Friends?"

I know a couple of mothers who had seasons of loss after loss in their family. For one mother, her father had suffered a serious stroke, their only calf had died, chickens had died, and worst of all, their baby boy died unexpectedly. But that wasn't the end of it. There was severe sickness and emergency surgery; it seemed as if the string of tragedies would never come to an end. For another family, they lost their first baby, then their baby goats were eaten by a cougar, and other "misfortunes" happened all within a short timeframe.

When we go through tragedy and suffering, our faith is frequently shaken, and we wonder just how much God is going to allow.

I remember wondering the same thing after our two miscarriages and losing Serena. What was God going to do next? Would He ever allow me to have a living child? Would He keep dangling a baby in front of my face only to rip it out of my reach? It also terrified me to think that God had the power to keep every one of my babies alive, but for some reason, He didn't.

You may be feeling the same thing when tragedy after tragedy strikes: "God, You could have intervened. You could have chosen a different outcome. You could have done a miracle, just like You've done for so many others." And because He didn't come through with a miracle, you've started doubting whether He loves you or not, whether you had enough faith, whether He is punishing you for some unknown sin that you have done... the list goes on and on. The mental agony and torment are maddening. It is like a whirling tornado that sucks the life out of your mental faculties and after spinning you around in its tenacious funnel, leaves you hopeless and exhausted.

In this chapter, I want to focus on overcoming the "what will God do next" battle. As I mentioned earlier, this seems to be a completely natural response to endless tragedy, but at the same time, this is also an opportunity to really dig in deep and grow stronger in your faith and trust in the Lord. We have a choice as to how we will respond: Will we distrust God and back away from Him? Or, will we lean into Him and send our roots deep down into the ground, learning to trust Him despite how we feel? When everything is going well, and we only experience minor challenges few and far between, our trust in the Lord really doesn't get a chance to grow. But, by beginning to look at this as an opportunity to grow in our trust of the Lord, we can help fortify our mind when Satan comes with all of his devious tactics.

The next strategy in fighting this battle is to **focus on the fact that the Lord only allows suffering in our lives because He loves us.** We often look at suffering negatively, but as we just "panned a few nuggets" on suffering a few chapters ago, suffering is actually an instrument that God uses for our good. He uses it to refine, discipline and make us more like Him. Everything that He allows has a purpose and a specific design, whether for our lives, others' lives or lives to come.

When we see suffering as God doing a beautiful work in our life, instead of wondering, "What are you going to take next, God?" we can try to pray, "Lord, please help me to be open-handed to You. Help me to trust that You are working something beautiful in my life, and if it means taking everything away from me so that Your perfect work might be done in my life, please give me the grace to be victorious through it all that You might be glorified."

I understand that this takes a great deal of courage. I can't say that I was very strong or submissive to the will of the Lord. In fact, it was a slow journey of learning to trust that God's ways were best. It resembled a baby learning to walk: lots of falls, getting back up, wobbling, feeble steps and slow moving. It meant "taking every thought captive to obedience of Christ," and it meant making a concerted effort to focus on truth and not on the lies that Satan was whispering in my ear constantly.

Another battle strategy is **to look at everything that God has given to you as on loan from Him.** When we take a step back, we see that nothing truly belongs to us—we are simply stewards of what God has given to us. Though it can be excruciatingly painful when God takes it away from us, keeping the healthy perspective that everything we have truly belongs to the Lord and He has given it to us for as long as He deemed best helps to quiet our questioning whether God is being faithful, good and fair to us. When we train our hearts to be thankful for the time that we *did* have with our loved one, or for the opportunities we were given with whatever He had entrusted to our care, our perspective starts to shift. This change helps our hearts not to be knit so tightly to the temporal things of this world but instead focused on eternal things. This is not to say that we cannot (and should not) love deeply or value the things that the Lord gives us. It is just to encourage a healthy perspective, keeping God as our sufficiency and not valuing the gift more than the Giver.

Another strategy in handling this could be asking yourself, **"What profit is it if I sit here and become bitter against the Lord, wondering what He is going to do next? What if instead I grow closer to Him, and learn to trust Him better so that even if something awful happens again, I will be able to lean into Him and find the strength that I won't have any other way?"** In our fallen world, terrible things are going to happen, and in reality, it is only because of God's goodness to us that we are not constantly bombarded with the most wicked things imaginable. He restrains the evil that can happen in this world—evil that was because of our choice as mankind.

When He placed Adam and Eve in the Garden of Eden, He had created a perfect world for them, but He gave them free will. They could choose to obey God and live, or they could choose to disobey and die. Because of Adam and Eve's choice to disbelieve what God said, listen to the lies of Satan and distrust that He did not have their best in mind, all of mankind since has been destined to an eternity in hell, except for those whose hearts have been changed by the Holy Spirit and who have trusted in Him alone for salvation. So, ultimately, our tragedies are not God's fault but are the result of a fallen world. However, we are incredibly blessed that He has not left us to ourselves, to live in this sinful world and to die without hope. Because of His willingness to take many of us in as His children, He sent His Son to die—what looked like a tragedy—so that we could have life.

When we are tempted to question what God would allow next, maybe it would be helpful to instead think of how much God has actually saved us from and how much evil He has shielded us from every single day. When we start thinking about how God has not wronged us, and that we haven't experienced everything that we deserve because of original sin and rebellion against the Lord, it helps us cultivate a sense of gratitude. We see how much He has blessed us with, and we can move beyond distrusting God to realizing how great His love and care is for us. When we grasp this truth, we can comfort ourselves by saying, "This would have happened to me anyway. I can choose to either walk away from the Lord and navigate the troubles of this life *without* Him who has proved to me before that He is my shield, my Rock, my Fortress and my Strength. Or, I can choose to lean into Him, navigate these troubles *with* Him and use this pain as an opportunity to know His love, kindness, care and compassion in a way that I would never have experienced."

Trusting God after repeated tragedy strikes may seem completely impossible to do as a human, but when I am tempted to think this, my mind goes back to Job. We will look at Job in greater detail later, but for now, I hope that you can find encouragement from Job's response to tragedies striking him all on one day, including the loss of all his possessions and every one of his ten children: "Naked came I out of my mother's womb, and naked shall I return thither: the Lord gave, and the Lord hath taken away; blessed be the name of the Lord." (Job 1:21) When his health was taken away after everything else, he responded with "…shall we receive good at the hand of God, and shall we not receive evil?" (Job 2:12) Job's trust in the Lord was so deeply rooted that he said, "Though He slay me, yet will I trust in Him…" (Job 13:15) Yes, Job vacillated between strong faith and wondering what God was doing. He wished for death, but he also held on to the fact that "He knoweth the way that I take: when He hath tried me, I shall come forth as gold." (Job 23:10)

Job and other believers responded to deep suffering and pain in their lives by being honest and transparent with the Lord. They laid out their pain before Him along with all their questions, doubts, fears and anger, and yet they still clung to the truths that they knew about the Lord. They answered their doubts and fears with the truth of His character and memories of His faithfulness in the past. In the same way, I encourage you to bring your questions and turmoil to the Lord.

"Lord I see that You are bringing pain after pain in my life. I don't understand it, and I am overwhelmed by it. Lord, I honestly feel like I can't take anymore, and to be completely blunt, I am utterly scared that You are going to take everything from me. I am terrified that You are going to never give me another child. You may take my spouse, my other children, my job, my house, my dog, my money, my parents, my siblings, my friends, everything. And, Lord, I really don't know how I can survive without any of them.

But, Lord, I know that You need to be my All in all, that I need to be content with only You if that is what You think is best in order to make me more like You. Please use all of these tragedies to make me a beacon of light and hope to the world around me. Please don't allow bitterness to well up in my heart against You, but give me the grace to thank You for every one of these tragedies. Show me how to use this pain to bring Your message of salvation and hope to those around me. Give me Your eyes to see that even though You bring trial after trial into my life, You love me. It is because You love me so dearly that You have allowed not just one pain, but lots of pain. Touch me with Your healing hand and help me to know the blessedness of resting in quiet hope in the arms of the Balm of Gilead."

Chapter 26

Joseph's Story

Do you think it is impossible to go through this depth of pain and not become bitter or resentful? Do you wonder if you will ever love God with the same passion that you had before this tragedy, or if you will live in fear of His power and sovereignty for the rest of your life? Do you struggle with a victim mentality and wonder if it is possible to actually come out of this pain victorious and as a conqueror?

The story of Joseph was instrumental in helping me realize that there can be a "Yes!" to every one of these questions. When we are walking through the tunnel of sorrow and grief, it may seem impossible to come out of the other side victorious, but let's explore Joseph's life and see what his perspective was after years of injustice, suffering and pain.

Joseph was born into a household of competition. There were four wives to one man, and the women were constantly fretting about who would have more children (and be truly loved because of it). Joseph's father, Jacob, loved him more than the other ten sons that were born by the other three wives, and this made those brothers angry and jealous. They couldn't stand Joseph to begin with, and to make the jealousy even worse, Jacob gave Joseph a beautiful coat of many colors, signifying how special he was to him. Joseph began having dreams that seemed to indicate his family would be subordinate to him in the future. Of course, this infuriated his brothers even more.

One day, his father sent him out to check on his brothers, who were tending sheep far away. Long story short, the brothers plotted to kill him, as their hatred had grown exponentially. God orchestrated the events so that Joseph was sold as a slave to merchants who were passing by on their way to Egypt. Joseph was taken to a strange land, with strange gods and a strange language, to serve as a slave. He was sold to Potiphar, the captain of Pharaoh's guard, and did such a wonderful job of service that Potiphar put him in charge of everything and trusted him completely. God prospered Potiphar on account of Joseph.

It wasn't long before Potiphar's wife decided that Joseph was good material for an affair and overtly tried to seduce him. Joseph would not give in to her because of his fidelity to her husband, but more importantly, because he would not sin against God. One day, she grabbed him and told him to sleep with her, but instead of giving in to the temptation, he ran out the door, leaving his coat in her hand. She made up an elaborate story about how he was trying to assault her, telling the lie to the servants as well as her husband. As you would expect, Potiphar was exceedingly angry and immediately threw Joseph into prison.

Can you imagine how Joseph felt? First, he was sold as a slave and taken away from his family, his home, and everything he loved and knew. For all he knew, he would never see his father again.

It seems like he made the most of his situation and decided to be faithful in whatever place the Lord put him. So, as a slave in Potiphar's home, he did his absolute best and gained the trust of a heathen man. The Lord blessed and prospered him. He didn't give in to the seduction and temptation of his master's wife, as many would have. How easy would it have been to justify why it would be understandable for him to do so? But he would not sin against God nor betray his master. When she attempted to physically force him into sleeping with her, he ran away.

He could have thrown in the towel, saying, "What was the point? Look at where I am! I remained faithful to God. I didn't betray my master, and here I am in this prison for doing nothing wrong!" He could have asked himself over and over, "Why God? Why? I was faithful to You. I didn't give into temptation. I didn't betray my master. I shone as a light for You in this heathen home; so much that even he could see You were with me. Why did You allow this to happen?"

Perhaps he did feel this way. Perhaps he did experience tremendous turmoil in his soul and had to convince himself daily to continue to be faithful. Either way, instead of becoming bitter and resentful over the injustice he had suffered yet again, Joseph chose to make the most of the place where God's providence had placed him, as hard as it was. For all he knew, he wasn't ever getting out of prison after being accused of assaulting the captain of the guard's wife. But the Lord was on Joseph's side through it all.

The prison guard soon realized the Lord was with Joseph and set him in charge of all the prisoners. One day, Pharaoh's cupbearer and baker were thrown into prison and thus were put under the care of Joseph. Shortly after, they both had dreams. Joseph interpreted the dreams, and the interpretations came to pass. The baker was hanged, and the cupbearer was restored to his position. Joseph asked the cupbearer to make mention of him so that he could get out of the prison as he hadn't done anything to deserve imprisonment.

Did the cupbearer remember? No. Two whole years would pass before Joseph would be lifted out of prison in order to interpret Pharaoh's dreams. That was the moment when everything would change for Joseph. He became 2nd in command in Egypt and formulated a plan for Egypt to survive the coming famine. After seven years of abundance in the fields, the dreaded famine came, and it was then that Joseph would meet his brothers again. They didn't recognize him apart from being the ruler that they were coming to buy corn from, but he recognized them. After a series of tests to see what their state of heart was, he revealed himself to his dumbfounded brothers and invited them to bring his father, come down to Egypt and live there until the famine was over. After their father died, his brothers were afraid that he would avenge himself on them for the awful thing they did to him. But what was Joseph's response after all that he endured?

> *"And Joseph said unto them, Fear not:*
> *for am I in the place of God?*
>
> *But as for you, ye thought evil against me; but*
> *God meant it unto good, to bring to pass, as it*
> *is this day, to save much people alive."*

> —Genesis 50:19-20

What a beautiful glimpse into Joseph's heart! No bitterness. No resentment. No victim mentality. He simply acknowledged that they had intended evil and chose to focus on the fact that God had turned it into something good—a means of salvation.

And so, He can do the same for you. When you are tempted to doubt God's love because of the pain that you are going through; when you are tempted to question God's goodness; when you are tempted to walk away, remember the story of Joseph and how he didn't know the end of the story. Throughout all of those years, he was away from his home, serving in a strange country, then thrown in prison due to no fault of his own and forgotten by one that he had helped, he couldn't see what God would eventually do. **We** know the end of Joseph's story, but when he was going through it all, he didn't know how it would turn out. He remained faithful to the Lord, and he was eventually blessed to see the reason why God had allowed it all. He was the means used to preserve the nation of Israel through whom the Savior of the world would come.

You may not know what the end of your story holds, and it might be hard to believe it could bring about anything but heartache. But I hope you can be encouraged by the story of Joseph and see that God is working in your waiting, even when it seems like hope is lost.

May the Lord hold you fast as you go through the dark times now, and may He show you the blessing that He is going to bring through your suffering in the days to come.

Chapter 27

Maintaining Your Marriage, Even in Loss

When we lost Serena, I remember reading something that noted that the loss of a child can either tear a couple apart or bring them closer together. Thankfully, my husband and I bonded even more deeply with the loss of Serena, as well as after our miscarriage losses. However, this doesn't always happen with couples, and I just wanted to take some time to encourage those who are struggling in their relationship after a loss.

To be honest, I don't feel very adequate to encourage you since I personally didn't experience much tension in my marriage relationship compared to others' experience. However, I hope and pray that some of the following things I've learned will be of encouragement. I've compiled some truths about how people grieve as well as some things I have learned from a friend who did experience some challenges in her marital relationship following the death of their six-month-old daughter. May the Lord remind you that wherever you find your relationship now, you are not alone. He can use even these challenges to make you grow stronger.

1. **Everyone grieves differently.**

   Men grieve differently than women, and women grieve differently than men. Some people are more expressive in their grief, while others seek to conceal it. Some want to talk about their loss, and others just want to bury it.

   I remember a conversation with a friend of mine who lost her baby girl during labor three months prior to Serena's death. At the time of our conversation, we were both expecting another baby. I couldn't help but notice how she wanted to focus on the new pregnancy, even though our losses were only a year (or less) old. In fact, she didn't even mention the name of the baby she had lost when referring to her. On the other hand, I couldn't keep from talking about Serena, even though I was expecting another baby. We each represented two different ways of dealing with the loss of our babies.

   One of my friends wanted everything pertaining to her deceased baby taken and put away by the time they returned from the hospital. On the other hand, I wanted to keep the crib assembled and did so for months. We kept it up until we moved and then set it up again months before our next baby would be born.

2. **People come from all sorts of different backgrounds.**

   This affects how they grieve as well. On the first anniversary of Serena's death, I had assumed that my husband would go with me to the cemetery where we would place flowers in her memory. When I spoke to him about it the night before, he showed some hesitation about going. I confess that I was really hurt by this. How could he not want to go to the cemetery?! His hesitation added to the already overwhelming grief that I felt. I asked him the next morning what it was that caused his reluctance, and he revealed he wasn't sure that he could actually handle it. He comes from a family where emotions were stifled and not freely expressed, whereas I come from a family where we were encouraged to face our emotions and deal with them head-on. Mourning and grief weren't concealed in my father's culture, whereas in the culture my husband grew up in, grief was not something you really showed.

3. **Life experience.**

This can also affect how someone deals with the loss of a child. Some have experienced loss already; others haven't experienced loss at all. Some have experienced expected losses; others have experienced unexpected losses. Some have had a hard childhood, while others have had a relatively easy childhood. All of these things could factor into how someone deals with the devastation of loss.

4. **Spiritual strength.**

Spiritual strength can be another factor in determining how someone handles the loss of a child. While I felt that I was strong spiritually and had been well-grounded in my faith, having a lot of Biblical knowledge and being well-versed in doctrine, I realized just how much of that needed to make the journey from my head into my heart. There were lessons that I needed to learn; lessons that my husband had already learned and grasped, so he was able to deal with the loss in a different way than I did. My husband didn't struggle with the question of whether things were fair or not, or how God dealt with us as opposed to others. He also seemed to accept God's plan a lot more readily than I did. He was very patient with me as I struggled and waffled, bouncing back and forth between what I knew in my head and what I was feeling in my heart. If you are on the other side of this and your spouse is the one who is really struggling, please know how grateful we are that you deal patiently with us and love us unconditionally as we painstakingly learn these lessons through suffering.

5. **Personalities.**

A person's personality can also affect the way one suffers. One of my friends spoke of how she had begun grieving for their son from week 28 and onward when they discovered that he had a heart defect and likely wouldn't survive birth. Her husband, on the other hand, had kept up hope all the way to the end of the pregnancy and didn't really start grieving until six months later. There are those who tend to look at life from the "cup half-empty" perspective. These personalities will tend to look at everything through the lenses of how they are being wronged and how unjust it seems. They can't really see much beyond all the pain and devastation they are drowning in.

For those who tend to look at life from the "cup half-full" perspective, while they might fall into grief every now and then, they will more commonly be found being thankful for the good things that have happened and focusing on living life again rather than dwelling in the past. You may find them saying something like, "Well, I can't change what happened; so I am just going to learn how to make lemonade with the lemons." This can be really frustrating and irritating for someone who is feeling like they are suffocating in their pain, so please be aware of how differences in your personalities can affect the grieving process.

6. **Present circumstances** in life also affect how one handles grief. Pressures with work and business, family issues, hospital bills, and so much more can play a part in how each spouse approaches the healing process.

7. **Different occasions in life will bring up the pain in different ways.**

   I remember attending a wedding nearly a year after Serena's death. Before the ceremony, there was a slideshow on display. Little did I realize how seeing the photos of the bride—the firstborn daughter—as a baby with her mother would reopen the wound in my heart and bring fresh tears that I fought to conceal with every ounce of willpower. It struck me anew that I wouldn't have any happy photos with my firstborn daughter.

   Another memory I have is while working on a yard project. As I heaved the shovelfuls of dirt, I kept repeating in my mind, "You're almost there! Almost there! You can do it! Just a little more!" Suddenly, I stopped mid-shovel. It was those same words that were repeated to me over and over throughout my long and difficult labor with Serena. Another flood of tears came rushing back. Sometimes grief hits at the most unexpected times.

A few things which may be helpful to remember, that are more pertinent to you both as a couple, are:

1. **Just because your spouse doesn't grieve the same way as you doesn't mean he/she isn't hurting as you are or that they don't love your child in the same way.**

   About two or so years after we lost Serena, I was working at an event with my husband and assisting some of his employees with a task that needed to be accomplished. As we sat there working on the project, the subject of Serena came up with one of the employees, who was in his early 60s. He then opened up and shared with me his family's story. He and his wife had six children, and years ago, for the first time since they had had children, they decided to go away together for a weekend and left the children with the grandparents. While they were gone, their youngest son died from SIDS. Immediately, they packed up and returned home. He spoke of how they went to a support group with other parents who had lost children, and how his wife would just talk and talk about it and cry and share with the other women. He, on the other hand, didn't want to say much about it at all. He told me that maybe all the talking she did was really good for her, because she is doing very well 20+ years later. On the contrary, he starts weeping when certain songs on the radio come on and trigger memories. This showed me that while our husbands may not show their grief, the pain is deep within them too.

2. **Perhaps your spouse feels that they need to be strong for you so that their grief doesn't burden you.**

   I remember my husband breaking down in the hospital when we discovered that Serena's heart was no longer beating. Almost as quickly as the breakdown came, it was over. It was like he tried to compose himself and said, "I'm sorry;

I need to be strong for you." I recall him saying this another time as well, and I encouraged him not to bury his grief in order to be strong for me. I needed him to know I was okay with the fact that he too was grieving for our daughter.

3. **Oftentimes husbands feel like they need to fix the problem for their wives.**

   Many times, husbands, as the protectors of the home, feel that they need to fix a problem that their wife is experiencing. However, in doing so, it could actually make the problem even worse. Of course, they aren't intending that, but sometimes we, as wives, desire to pour our hearts out to our husbands. We just need him to listen and not try to "fix" the problem. When he attempts to fix it, oftentimes, it can come across as a lack of sympathy, understanding or compassion. This can cause the wife to explode, withdraw or become resentful, which only adds to the hurricane of emotions that is whirling about with loss. On the other hand, wives may try to draw out the emotions of their husbands. We might try to figure out every detail of what they are feeling, causing our husbands to feel trapped or pressured.

A few things that may be crucial in helping you grow closer during this tough time are:

1. **Communication:** this is the #1 thing I hear concerning spouses dealing with loss. If something is bothering you or your spouse, or you are having a "bad" day, tell each other so that you can support one another and count on each other no matter what. Don't bottle it in! Keeping it in only adds to the burden that you are already carrying and puts a wedge in between both of you.

2. **Try to get some time away as just the two of you.** If you have other children to care for, work demands and pressures on top of all the regular challenges of life, it can be easy for you both to drift apart as you grieve. If you are both busy, you may start to grieve independently because it feels like there is no time to process through it all. Time away can give you some space to focus on each other and talk through how you are both processing the loss. You will have the opportunity to take the time to share the deep feelings of your hearts, allowing you to understand each other better. Sometimes comments are made in the everyday that are not intended to be hurtful, but because of the stress of the loss of a child, they are received as such and can begin to put a wedge between you. Share these instances with your spouse, making sure not to come across as accusatory but saying something like, "When you said... I felt..." Approaching the conversation this way takes the blame off of them, but also lets them know that you were hurt by what was said.

3. **Try to talk about grief on "good days."** This means waiting to talk about your loss until the days when the pain is not so acute, or when you are feeling a little more positive. Perhaps you can come up with an action plan that works for both of your needs when you are having a bad day. For example, if you, the wife, feel that all you need is to cry in your husband's arms as you pour out your heart and get reassurance of his love and care, it would be good to communicate this to your husband. This gives him an opportunity to have a clear picture of the kind of support you need. On the other hand, if your husband feels that he

needs to go out and play a round of basketball or go for a jog/hike, it would be beneficial for him to communicate this to you so you can have a clear picture of the kind of support he needs. This way, when that "bad day" hits, both of you will know how to best minister to each other in a way that makes the other feel loved and supported.

4. **Remember that this is a journey.** Both of you will be learning things every week, every day, every hour and every moment. Lessons take time to learn. Often, we wish we could just learn the lesson and move on! It would make things so much easier. But profound lessons take a lot of time, energy, effort and oftentimes, pain.

5. **Don't put a timeline on grief.** I have spoken about this previously, but thought it was worth mentioning again here as we often feel like we should be "over" this already. When grief overwhelms us day after day and sucks the life and joy out of us, it is easy to wonder when this grieving process will ever end (and *if* it will ever end). But remember to give yourself time. There isn't a specific timeline that you must fit into or follow. God works with everyone at their own pace.

6. **Be patient with yourself and with your spouse.** You both will heal at different paces. Perhaps thinking of it as a marathon could help. It is rare for couples to have the same strengths and weaknesses in running. One of you could be great at the flat terrain; the other could be better on the uphill climbs. One could have that "off like a speeding bullet" type of energy, while the other could be steady and constant. You can choose to run solo, in keeping with your own strengths and weaknesses and leave your spouse to do the same… or you can choose to run together, hand in

hand, so that when one is having a hard time on the hills, the other can help. And when the other is having a hard time enduring and getting across the finish line, the other can encourage and inspire.

7. **Humility goes a long way in maintaining your relationship.** Being willing to say, "I am sorry," and to admit that you weren't sympathetic, understanding, self-sacrificial or loving helps to restore ground that was lost in the journey of grief. When one excuses their behavior because they are grieving, and expects everyone to excuse whatever they do or say because they lost a child, relationships cannot thrive. It is true, you are grieving—and you are grieving one of the most painful experiences in life, one that is contrary to nature (it isn't natural or expected to bury one's child as it is natural or expected to bury one's parents). However, grief cannot become an excuse for unloving behavior. I remember a situation with my aunts where they made some very insensitive comments during the time I was expecting Caleb. I completely lost it with them. Even though their comments were incredibly hurtful, and felt as if they were reopening wounds that had begun to heal, it didn't excuse my response. After I had time to reflect on it, I apologized to them for my un-Christ-like response and our relationship was restored rather than permanently damaged.

8. **Ultimately, your spouse cannot give you everything you need for comfort during this loss.** While having a spouse to walk through the loss with is a wonderful gift from the Lord, it is important to distinguish that they are not a replacement for what the Lord only can give. He *alone* can bind up your aching heart. He *alone* can soothe the stinging pain. He *alone* can provide the peace that passes all understanding. He *alone*

can cause you to see the good that can come out of devastation and anguish. If you look to your spouse to be everything to you in the middle of your pain, you are actually placing a burden on them that they simply cannot bear. They were not designed to bear that burden as a mere human being—that is for the Lord, and the Lord alone, to bear. Finding the balance is a hard thing to do, but asking the Lord to help me has always been a tremendous aid when I am having a hard time figuring out how much to lean on my husband.

I hope that some of the things that I have suggested will be helpful to you both as you navigate this journey of grief together. I pray that the Lord will use this tragedy to bind you closer together and to Him. Keep Him as the solid foundation for your marriage and remember that He gave you to each other to help you weather the storms of life. Together you are stronger. Our wedding passage came from Ecclesiastes 4:9-12 and is a good reminder of how God intends couples to be stronger together:

> *"Two are better than one; because they*
> *have a good reward for their labor.*
>
> *For if they fall, the one will lift up his fellow:*
> *but woe to him that is alone when he falleth;*
> *for he hath not another to help him up…*
>
> *And if one prevail against him, two shall withstand*
> *him; and a threefold cord is not quickly broken."*

Remember that you are in this together and you *can* come through it together. Intertwine your hearts together with the strong cord of Christ, and you will find a strength that you never thought was possible.

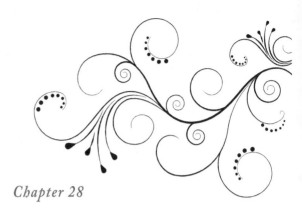

Chapter 28

Seven-Month Birthday

Dear grieving mother,

Another month has passed, and in the blink of an eye, seven months have gone by. Perhaps you are feeling like no one remembers your little one anymore. You long to talk about them, to hear their name, to know that someone remembers they existed; but unless you bring it up, your precious child's name is not uttered.

Dear one, remember that most people don't really know what to say. Even if they do, they may be afraid that if they mention your child's name, it will bring a fresh flood of tears. What they don't know is that those tears would be both tears of sadness and joy, simply because someone cared enough to let us know they still think of our precious one.

I encourage you to take the initiative: Step out of your grief for a moment and talk about your little one. Share the dreams, hopes, and memories you have with someone that you can trust. Let others know that you don't mind talking about your child, and that the tears are okay too.

Perhaps you may also be struggling with a lack of desire to do what you know is right. As every day brings you farther away from the last moment you held your dear one, and closer to the one-year mark, you may find that it is easier to pick up the pieces of your dramatically changed life now as you aren't as overwhelmed by the grief which clouded everything. However, amidst all of the circumstantial change, something inside you has changed too—you feel a distance from the Lord.

For what seemed like months on end, you have been battling doubt, fear, and a tornado of other emotions that have spun you around. Now that the storm may have subsided, the unusual silence is almost terrifying. Satan may be trying a different tactic. Rather than bombarding you with a plethora of fiery darts, he tries the tactic of apathy. You may find that you have no desire to pray, read the Scriptures, attend church, or reach out to others. You may start noticing a nonchalant feeling creeping in about your spiritual state that can leave you more petrified than when you were battling fiercely day after day. You may be waiting for the feelings of love, trust, faith, and zeal to envelop you, but day after day, there is no change. Perhaps you feel that it would be hypocritical to engage in any spiritual activities without having your heart truly in it.

If you are struggling with this, I encourage you to once again throw yourself at the feet of Jesus. Tell Him that you don't feel like praying, that you don't feel like reading His Word, and that you don't feel like attending His worship or fellowshipping with believers. Tell Him that you don't feel like loving Him, and you don't feel like He is worthy of your trust. Tell Him that you don't feel like your faith in Him is well-grounded anymore. Tell Him that you don't want to do the right thing; that you don't want to forgive or attempt to move past your tragedy, and that you would like to sit in the mire and be a victim of your pain. Tell Him that you have no feelings to do what you know He asks you to do.

Then, ask Him to restore the joy of His salvation to you. Ask Him to renew a right spirit within you. Ask Him to give you a burning zeal in your heart for His service and kingdom and then, don't stop there. Get up and do what you know is right. Choose to love Him even when you don't feel like it. Choose to trust Him even when you feel like He failed you. Choose to have faith that He is doing what is best for you, even when you don't understand. Choose to attend His worship and fellowship with His people. Choose to read His Word even when you have no desire to do so. Choose to reach out to those who are hurting and become the arms and feet of Jesus to them. Choose to apologize when you have wronged others.

Please know that this is not hypocrisy. It is living faith and obedience to the Lord. As you follow what the Lord says instead of your feelings, the feelings will follow. God will bless you for obeying Him despite your swirling emotions, and you will find greater depth in your relationship with the Lord—one that is truly faith-based and not based on feelings.

May Jesus wrap you tightly in His arms today and let you know just how much He loves you and your little one, igniting the zeal in your heart for His kingdom and restoring to you, once again, the joy of His salvation.

Chapter 29

Responding to Crisis

This morning, I heard a wonderful sermon which had a few points in it that I thought were helpful to apply to my own life in experiencing loss. As I wrote a few of the main takeaways down, I thought it might be beneficial for other bereaved mothers to hear as well.

The main point from the sermon was about how we respond to crisis in our lives. Principles were taken from the story of Jairus (and his daughter) and the woman who had the issue of blood. Just in case you aren't familiar with the story of Jairus, I will give a short summary. A ruler of the synagogue, Jairus, had a twelve-year-old daughter who was very sick. He went out to find Jesus, asking Him to come and heal his daughter. Jesus agreed to go to his house, but as Jesus went, multitudes started thronging Him. One of the people in the crowd was a woman who had an issue of blood for twelve years. She had spent all that she had on doctors—who we think could have solved the problem—but instead of getting better, she was getting worse. In faith, she decided to touch the hem of Jesus' garment as He made His way through the crowds to Jairus' house.

Immediately, her flow of blood stopped and Jesus noticed that power had gone out of Him. He stopped in the crowd and asked, "Who touched Me?" The disciples were incredulous. "Lord, You see the multitudes thronging, and You ask, 'Who touched Me?'" Jesus continued to look around until the woman came forward and explained her story. He said to her, "Daughter, your faith has healed you; go in peace." In the meantime, someone came to Jairus and told him that there was no point in having Jesus come to the house. His daughter had died. You can likely imagine how Jairus must have felt at that moment. I am sure many of us would have been ready to scream our lungs out at the woman who delayed Christ with her issue. We would have been envious that her problem was solved while our daughter was dead.

Our pastor spoke of how we can have a victim mentality—thinking that everything and everyone has to be put to the side because of the crisis in our own lives. Jairus could have experienced the same thing; throwing a pity party because this woman was healed of her issue while his daughter died because of the delay. When we lose a child, it can so consume our thoughts and emotions that we are prone to fall into this victim mentality. We feel that others' problems are not as big as ours. We expect them to reach out to us, and we expect their lives to stop just as ours stopped the moment our child's heartbeat did.

Our pastor spoke of how we can harbor resentment towards family, friends, and acquaintances who don't give us everything that we expect when we are going through a crisis, but have we stopped to consider that they may be going through a crisis of their own? Jairus may have experienced anger and resentment against the woman for delaying Jesus, yet this woman had suffered from a constant hemorrhaging for twelve years—the entire length of his daughter's life. Due to the Levitical laws of the time, she was basically cut off from society as she was perpetually unclean. She wouldn't have been permitted to attend the worship of the Lord, and anyone or anything she touched would have been considered unclean. She likely lived a very lonely life, not to mention the fact that she would be growing weaker and weaker, and likely anemic, with the constant loss of blood. We often expect people to cut us some slack because of what we are going through, but have we stopped to consider that they may be going through something that we aren't aware of, and they are also in need of our understanding?

He exhorted us not to be mute while trudging through it. Sometimes, we don't share our struggles or that which we are going through, yet we expect people just to reach out and help us even though they are unaware of the situation or that we are actually struggling. Oftentimes, people who have not experienced loss don't know what to say, or they are clueless as to how long the anguish continues and how deep the pain really is. Without us sharing it, how can we expect them to reach out to us and come alongside us to help? How can we expect them to understand something they have never been through? At the same time, because they haven't been through the loss of a child, they may not be the best candidates for helping us, so let us refrain from laying blame on them when they aren't able to assist us simply because they cannot.

Our pastor urged us to believe God's promises and take hold of them in faith, no matter how long it takes for them to be fulfilled. As Jesus reminded Jairus, "Be not afraid, only believe," so we can be encouraged to hold onto His promises to us in faith. Instead of resenting Christ for ministering to others in their crisis while it appears that He has delayed in ministering to us in *our* pain, rejoice that He has answered the prayers of others and wait in expectation for His answer to your prayers. He is faithful to His promises, and He will be faithful to you.

Finally, he spoke of how our crisis never outvalues the kingdom of God. Don't push away opportunities to advance the kingdom during your time of crisis. From personal experience, I found that reaching out to others in their struggles, no matter how weak and exhausted I was with my own grief, helped to heal my heart and find purpose in the plan that God had for our lives. I also found that when I kept my focus on Christ, it was easier to calm the resentment and bitterness that threatened to come in when others didn't respond as I expected them to. When I find myself falling prey to a victim mentality, remembering that Jesus sees, cares, remembers and went through the greatest crisis on earth so that my little girl could be in heaven—safe, perfect, and forever in eternal serenity—helps my heart to quiet once again. This remembrance allows my perspective to reflect more of my heavenly Father.

I encourage you, dear mother, to lay hold of Christ and ask Him for the grace to respond to others in a way that would please the Lord, even as you are broken with grief yourself.

Chapter 30

Trusting and Waiting on the Lord, Even in the Darkness

*"Who is among you that feareth the LORD,
that obeyeth the voice of His servant, that
walketh in darkness and hath no light?*

Let him trust in the name of the Lord and stay upon his God."

—Isaiah 50:10

In the days, weeks and months following Serena's death, this verse was a rock that anchored me during the turbulent waves and storms that roared in my soul. It gave me comfort because it spoke to the fact that there are those who do fear the Lord, who are obeying the commands of God, and yet they are still walking through darkness. They are experiencing sorrow and pain. They don't see any light at the end of the tunnel. They are in a dark valley, and they can't see the glorious mountaintop. They don't see the end of the rainstorm. There is no indication that the sun will ever shine again for them.

But, God brings encouragement in the midst of the darkness. He gives us direction to simply trust in His name. He encourages us to stay upon Him. In the Hebrew, to "stay" means to support one's self, to lean, and to rely on. Instead of relying on one's self to get through this difficult time, instead of relying on others' support, comfort and abilities, the Lord tells us that we need to be leaning on Him. He desires that we would be solely relying on and focusing on Him. Don't get me wrong; it is often a day-by-day leaning on Him. Sometimes it is even minute-by-minute or hour-by-hour.

Still, we want to see the end of the story. We want to know just how long this trial is going to last. We want to know the outcome *right now*. But, oftentimes, God calls us to wait, day after day. As we trust in Him for our daily sustenance, we learn reliance on Him that we would never know without this practical "in-the-trenches" lesson. This reliance will make us stronger in Christ and give us steadfastness in times of trouble that will be incomprehensible.

Contrary to what our flesh would tell us, the waiting makes us stronger, not weaker. As we wait, God is refining our character and teaching us many valuable lessons, one of them being humility—knowing that He is in control and not us. As we wait, our hope grows, and spiritual transformation begins. When the waiting gets to be too long, remember that Jesus had to wait until the right time for His suffering, crucifixion, and death. He also had to wait for His resurrection. As you wait, seek contentment in God's will, even though the circumstances are not anything close to what you would have dreamed of.

I pray that the Lord would meet you today in your pain and tears and that as you walk through the darkness without even the dim light of a candle, you would trust in Him, lean upon Him and rely on Him alone. I hope you are encouraged that you are not alone—there are many other servants of the Lord, who fear Him and who obey Him, and who are yet experiencing these dark times. But, be encouraged—light **will** come! "...weeping may endure for a night, but joy cometh in the morning." (Psalm 30:5)

It may be a very long "night," but the Lord **will** bring joy.

DAY BY DAY AND WITH EACH PASSING MOMENT

BY LINA SANDELL

Day by day and with each passing moment,
Strength I find to meet my trials here;
Trusting in my Father's wise bestowment,
I've no cause for worry or for fear.
He whose heart is kind beyond all measure
Gives unto each day what He deems best—
Lovingly, it's part of pain and pleasure,
Mingling toil with peace and rest.

Every day the Lord Himself is near me
With a special mercy for each hour;
All my cares He fain would bear, and cheer me,
He whose name is Counselor and Power.
The protection of His child and treasure
Is a charge that on Himself He laid;
"As thy days, thy strength shall be in measure,"

This the pledge to me He made.

Help me then in every tribulation
So to trust Thy promises, O Lord,
That I lose not faith's sweet consolation
Offered me within Thy holy Word.
Help me, Lord, when toil and trouble meeting,
E'er to take, as from a father's hand,
One by one, the days, the moments fleeting,
Till I reach the promised land.

Chapter 31

ℋℐ𝒮 *Purpose for Our Trials*

In this chapter, I would like to share the July 28th excerpt from Oswald Chambers' *My Utmost for His Highest*.

Note: I have emphasized the thoughts that were most helpful for me as I walked the path of grief.

> *"He made His disciples get into the boat and go before Him to the other side..." (Mark 6:45)*

We tend to think that if Jesus Christ compels us to do something and we are obedient to Him, He will lead us to great success. We should never have the thought that our dreams of success are God's purpose for us. In fact, His purpose may be exactly the opposite. We have the idea that God is leading us toward a particular end or a desired goal, but He is not. The question of whether or not we arrive at a particular goal is of little importance, and reaching it becomes merely an episode along the way. What we see as only the process of reaching a particular end, God sees as the goal itself.

What is my vision of God's purpose for me? Whatever it may be, His purpose is for me to depend on Him and on His power now. *If I can stay calm, faithful and unconfused while in the middle of the turmoil of life, the goal of the purpose of God is being accomplished in me. God is not working toward a particular finish- His purpose is the process itself. What He desires for me is that I see "Him walking on the sea" with no shore, no success, nor goal in sight, but simply having the absolute certainty that everything is all right because I see "Him walking on the sea" (6:49). It is the process, not the outcome, that is glorifying to God.*

God's training is for now, not later. His purpose is for this very minute, not for some time in the future. We have nothing to do with what will follow our obedience, and we are wrong to concern ourselves with it. What people call preparation, God sees as the goal itself.

God's purpose is to enable me to see that He can walk on the storms of my life right now. If we have a further goal in mind, we are not paying enough attention to the present time. However, if we realize that moment-by-moment obedience is the goal, then each moment as it comes is precious.

I hope that you found this reading to be as encouraging as I found it when we lost Serena. As I battled the raging waves of doubt and fear, anger and despair, it was such a comfort to me to know that Christ was there, walking on the waves. Even more encouraging was the fact that I could walk on those waves *with Him* if I simply kept my eyes fixed upon Him. It wasn't something utterly impossible.

It was helpful to me to remember that God had a purpose in these storms; the fact that they didn't take Him by surprise or were a "hiccup" in His plan was encouraging to me. He knew from the beginning that part of my story would include losing babies to miscarriage and my first full-term baby girl to death. This was all part of the plan that He had for my life. Did I understand it? Definitely not back then, but as the years have passed, I have gradually been able to see how His plan is like a beautiful tapestry in which He has made beauty from ashes.

To know that the goal of the purpose of God was being accomplished in me if I learned to remain calm, faithful, and unconfused amidst the waves that tossed me about helped to bring purpose to the pain and suffering. I pray that the same will be for you—that you will be able to see that the pain and suffering that God has allowed is not a surprise or a "hiccup" in God's plan. Rather, it is part of the goal that God has for your life in teaching you how to walk hand-in-hand with Him on the stormy waves with a sense of calm and peace that defies the storm around you.

Chapter 32

Eight-Month Birthday

Dear grieving mother,

How are you doing? Have you been experiencing waves of grief? Perhaps some days it seems like you have come to the place where you can live a somewhat normal life. Other days, you find yourself sinking in despair and hopelessness. Perhaps you have been reflecting on what life was like before tragedy hit, thinking about how glorious it was and why it couldn't stay that way.

We may never have answers to the questions that often come to our minds, but we can be encouraged that Jesus experienced the valleys as well. Philippians says that He learned obedience by the things that He suffered.

The following is a poem that I had been acquainted with a long time ago. It came back to my remembrance when I felt like I was in a dark valley following the death of Serena, and it ministered to my heart right where it was. I hope it can bring comfort and encouragement to you today on your journey as well.

IT'S IN THE VALLEYS I GROW
BY JANE EGGLESTON

Sometimes life seems hard to bear,
Full of sorrow, trouble and woe
It's then I have to remember
That it's in the valleys I grow.

If I always stayed on the mountain top
And never experienced pain,
I would never appreciate God's love
And would be living in vain.

I have so much to learn
And my growth is very slow,
Sometimes I need the mountain tops,
But it's in the valleys I grow.

I do not always understand
Why things happen as they do,
But I am very sure of one thing.
My Lord will see me through.

My little valleys are nothing
When I picture Christ on the cross

He went through the valley of death;
His victory was Satan's loss.

Forgive me Lord, for complaining
When I'm feeling so very low.
Just give me a gentle reminder
That it's in the valleys I grow.

Continue to strengthen me, Lord
And use my life each day
To share Your love with others
And help them find their way.

Thank You for valleys, Lord
For this one thing I know
The mountain tops are glorious
But it's in the valleys I grow!

Chapter 33

Job's Story

Our son recently achieved a great accomplishment, and as his reward, he chose the Bible storybook of Job. As our five children huddled around me to hear the new story, I realized just how much this story ministered to my heart in those days after we lost Serena. Even though we have spoken on the life of this great Bible hero previously, I felt the Lord spoke to me clearly through this children's book, and I want to specifically focus on how a few principles or verses can apply to the situation we find ourselves in.

1. Job was described as a "perfect and upright" man, "one who feared God, and eschewed evil." And yet, as we read the story, he was not exempt from trouble and devastation of the greatest kind. Not only was all his wealth taken from him in the matter of a day (the oxen were stolen, the sheep were burned up with fire from God, the camels were captured, and the servants that tended these animals all died except for one from each group), all ten of his children died on the same day! If you ever feel like you are getting

hit with one bad thing after another, Job could definitely identify with the same feeling.

2. Despite all the tragedy happening in a day, Job "fell down upon the ground and worshipped." Yes, he grieved. Yes, he was hurting. Yes, his heart was filled with anguish, yet, he worshipped. "Naked came I out of my mother's womb, and naked shall I return thither: the Lord gave, and the Lord hath taken away; blessed be the name of the Lord." I am always amazed at Job's response. He recognized that all he had—including his wealth and his children—belonged to the Lord and that it was His to give and His to take away. Everything was a gift, and if the Lord chose to take it away, Job would still bless the Lord.

3. When Job is struck with boils that covered his entire body, he had no solace or comfort from she who was to be his closest companion—his wife. Instead of encouraging him to trust in the Lord, or grieving with him in silence as his friends did in the very beginning, she said, "Dost thou still retain thine integrity? Curse God and die." How often have you felt like those who should help you through this devastating time actually tempt you to sin by the comments that they make? Job could relate to this as well.

4. Then, when three of his friends come, they sit in silence for seven days. But, after those initial seven days are over, they start berating Job and accusing him of some secret hidden sin, stating that this was the cause for his misfortune and calamity. Have you ever felt like your friends have quoted Scripture to you, or slammed theological doctrine in your face in an attempt to try to help you make sense of all that

you feel, only leaving you more helpless, discouraged, and desolate? Job knew this pain just as well.

5. The feelings of Job that are expressed throughout the book could be just the kinds of things that you are feeling:

    *   Why was I born? I wish I were never born.

    *   The thing that I greatly feared has come upon me.

    *   Please, Lord, just let me die!

    *   I feel like God is against me.

    *   Yes, I know I am a sinner.

    *   Lord, why are You doing this to me?

    *   All of you are miserable comforters.

    *   Have pity on me, O my friends; why are you persecuting me?

    *   Why do the wicked prosper and seem not to have any calamity come to them?

    *   Oh, that I could speak face to face with God!

    *   I thought I did all the right things.

    *   I have been put to shame by all of this.

6. And even in these dark times for Job, he made some of the strongest statements of truth, and some of the most steadfast confessions of faith.

    "For I know that my Redeemer liveth, and that He shall stand at the latter day upon the earth and though after my skin worms destroy this body, yet in my flesh shall I see God."

    "But He is in one mind, and who can turn Him? And what

His soul desireth, even that He doeth. For He performeth the thing that is appointed for me: and many such things are with Him."

"But He knoweth the way that I take: when He hath tried me, I shall come forth as gold."

"Though He slay me, yet will I trust in Him…"

7. The Lord comes to Job and speaks to him, causing Job to repent for speaking of things that he didn't truly understand. He realized just how small he was in comparison to the Lord.

8. The Lord hadn't overlooked the way in which Job's friends had treated him. In fact, His wrath was kindled against them. I always found it interesting that God told them to go to Job and Job would pray for them. How hard do we find it sometimes to pray for the Lord to forgive those who have poured salt into our wounds by their words and actions? Doesn't it feel easier sometimes to just "stew about it" or retaliate by giving them the silent treatment, engaging in a shouting match, gossip, withdrawing, or "pushing their buttons"? But I love how the Scriptures say, "And the Lord turned the captivity of Job, when he prayed for his friends." Remembering to take my focus off of the insult or injury done and rather focusing on my duty to pray for those who hurt me helps heal the wounds and keeps me in an open relationship with the Lord.

9. Also, the Lord gave Job twice as much as he had before. Isn't that amazing?! The Lord can do above that which we ask or think. I am sure Job didn't think about the fact that he would be doubly rich when he was sitting on the ash

heap, scraping his sore boils with a broken piece of pottery. He could only see the devastation, pain, anguish, and despair. But we now have this wonderful story to lift us up; to give us hope that the Lord **will** restore the years that the locusts have eaten, and that He can do so much more than we could ever expect.

May the story of Job comfort your heart today as you grapple with the questions, fight the doubts, face the Giant of Despair, struggle in the Slough of Despond and feel like you are fighting Apollyon. Remember that the Lord can do great things for you just as He did for Job. Cling to Him in faith. Keep your focus on Him. Repeat the truths that you know to yourself and wait in expectation to see how God will answer your prayers.

"Though He slay me, yet will I trust in Him…"

—Job 13:15

Chapter 34

Worship God for Who He Is, Not for What He Gives

As I think back to the time when we lost Serena and experienced miscarriages, a prominent truth that the Lord kept bringing to my mind was my need to worship God for who He is and not for what He does for us. It is easy to have a vibrant, feel-good relationship with Jesus when everything is going just the way we want it; when all of our prayers are answered just the way we have asked, and everything happens in the timeframe that we would like. But when our dreams are decimated and our prayers seem unanswered, and instead of blessings, it seems like tragedy after tragedy comes in like a flood, do we still have that same vibrant relationship? Do we still have that elevated view of God and bask in His presence? Or do we start feeling anger, doubt, mistrust, and fear of God? Do we withdraw from Him, wondering whether we are wasting our time in following Him? Is it even worth it?

It seems to me that a key point in helping us to continue to worship the Lord for who He is and not for what we get from Him (even when disaster is happening all around) is to remember that we don't really deserve anything except an eternity in hell. It is easy for us to get into the mindset of, "I go to church regularly, I pray daily, I read my Bible, I minister to believers, I witness to unbelievers, so I should be all good." We think that because we have all of the checkmarks on our mental "Please God List," God should do precisely what we want Him to do for us.

But when our focus shifts from what we want from God to everything that He has already done for us—everything that He has saved us from, and everything that He now is to us—it is truly humbling. When we realize what it cost the Father to send His Son to save us from our deserved punishment in hell, what it cost the Son to leave His home in heaven in order to be the sacrifice for our sins, it can cause us to break down in tears because of the depth of His love for us. When we think of how we daily grieve the Spirit by our thoughts and actions, when we think on all of the grace and mercy, longsuffering and love that He shows us day by day as we miserably fail to live out the truth that He has taught us, we should be humbled.

Something else that came to mind as I pondered this idea of only worshipping God for what He gives is this: what would it be like if someone were only to love me because of what they could get from me and not because of who I am? What would my thoughts be toward that person? And yet, if I am only worshipping and following God for what He gives to me, am I not being just like that?

I am always encouraged as I read the Lord's praise of Job to Satan, "and still he holdeth fast his integrity, although thou movedst Me against him, to destroy him without cause." (Job 2:3) And what was the secret of Job's holding fast? We can learn from his words to his wife when she told him to simply curse God and die: he said to her, "What? Shall we receive good at the hand of God and not evil?" (Job 2:10) Job realized that if he were to accept good from God, he should also accept the evil that the Lord would allow.

Once again, this is not easy to do when you are in the middle of grieving the death of your precious little one. I found it was a choice that had to be made. Sometimes it was a daily choice, but as I brought this difficulty to Christ, asking for the grace to love and worship Him just for who He is, regardless of what He gives, He lifted me in His arms and helped me along the path. I pray that it will be the same for you if you find yourself struggling in the same way.

I happened across the song, "I'll Praise You in This Storm" by Casting Crowns a few months after Serena's death. I had dropped off my brother-in-law and his family at the airport, and the CD was in the player. This song came on immediately as I began the drive back home, and I felt it was not a coincidence. It completely spoke to my heart and I could identify with the brutal reality of the feelings and emotions that come through: how we thought God would have come and "saved the day," how we can hardly move on because we can barely sense the Lord's presence in the overwhelming pain and the intensity of the storm.

It speaks of only being able to hear God's voice in a whisper and then, because of God's mercy, being able to get back up and praise Him in the storm. Even though our heart has been torn apart, we can trust that He is who He declares He is, no matter what happens. God's kindness, love, and care shines through the lyrics, and I can't count the number of times I sat down at the piano and played my pain out, choking through the lyrics as tears coursed down my cheeks, clinging to the truth expressed in this song—to praise God in the storm and to worship Him for who He is, regardless of my circumstances.

Chapter 35

Focus on Christ, That He Might Be Glorified

Do you struggle with how to respond to the comments that people make which sting terribly rather than soothe your aching heart? Comments that are sometimes true, but don't help the situation:

"It was all a part of God's sovereign plan."

"All things work together for good."

"Be thankful for the children that you *do* have."

"You're young; you can have more."

"The child would likely have been handicapped, so it is actually God's mercy to you that it ended in miscarriage or a stillbirth."

"Be thankful that you survived the traumatic birth."

...and the list goes on and on. It is so easy to lash out in anger and hurt when people say these things to you, especially as you grapple with the questions that you have surrounding the loss you are grieving. It is hard to keep your lips sealed from spilling out the words you feel like retorting for their well-intended but insensitive comments.

Fast forward several years. You have been kind and loving, keeping quiet when those comments have resurfaced. You have silently borne the lack of acknowledging the burden you bear every year, every month, and every day. You have smiled kindly when people have just not understood what it is like. And yet the more you have responded in a manner that imitates Christ, at times it seems like they take even more advantage. They still don't "get it." Somehow you have thought that the kindness, consideration, lack of revenge, and forgiveness you have portrayed will cause them to realize the burden you bear. Somehow you thought that perhaps they would come alongside you and help you shoulder it just once in a while, but alas! You have been mistaken. The lack of consideration and thoughtlessness remains.

Do you feel like your kind responses have been in vain? That you have silently borne this grief for nothing? Do you feel like next time a comment is made (or not made), you will just set them straight and give them a tongue lashing because the kind and quiet response hasn't seemed to work?

Something that I have been learning in several areas of life is keeping my focus on Christ. As long as my eyes are fixed on Him, no matter what someone does or doesn't do, I will have peace. Just as Peter could walk on the water as long as his eyes were on Jesus, we can walk on the waves and the stormy seas that threaten to shake and overwhelm us. As soon as we start focusing on the storm around us, it is impossible to feel such calm in our soul while experiencing the devastation we have been through. When we take our eyes off of Christ and His glory, turning our focus on ourselves and what we think are our rights, we begin to sink in those dark, awful waves that will overwhelm us in seconds. Thankfully, Jesus is right there, willing to stretch out His arm to us over and over again, pulling us up from drowning and bringing us back to the "boat"—a safe haven where we can refocus and fix our eyes upon Him again, worshipping Him for saving us.

If our focus remains on the Lord, and we are responding the way that He has graciously taught us in His Word, whether those around us ever understand or "get it" is not important anymore. The important thing is that Christ is glorified by our response and He is pleased when we have chosen to "turn the cheek" rather than "recompense evil for evil." He is pleased when we "follow after peace" and "put on the bowels of mercies and kindness." He is glorified when we forgive just as He has forgiven us.

May this treasure of keeping in mind that all we do is for Christ alone, regardless of how others respond, encourage you today on your journey through grief.

Chapter 36

Nine-Month Birthday

Dear grieving mother,

Nine months have gone by. Memories may be flooding your mind of what it was like last year as you were planning for the birth of your baby. You may have days where the grief hits out of nowhere, and other days where you feel like you can manage it well.

I would like to share a verse with you to bring encouragement in this storm.

> *"The righteous shall flourish like the palm tree:*
> *he shall grow like a cedar in Lebanon."*
>
> —Psalm 92:12

You may have heard this verse and thought it was a beautiful picture of God's promise of fruitfulness and growth and blessings for His people, but years ago, I heard something about the impact that storms have on palm trees that really resonated with me in the devastation. Many times, after a hurricane has wrought havoc in an area, the palm trees are seen to be still standing. How can they survive the storm?

Palm trees are designed so when the fierce storms come, they are able to bend and not break. Sometimes the winds are so severe that the trees are completely horizontal—parallel to the ground! But once the storm is over, they stand upright once again.

Not only that, but it has been found that the palm tree is actually stronger after the storm! The storm causes its roots to dig down deeper into the ground, and the trunk grows stronger. They grow taller and more beautiful. Another aspect to note is, the older a palm tree is and the more scarred it is, the sweeter the fruit will be.

What a beautiful picture to us when we are going through a time of devastation that makes us feel like we are so bent over with grief we feel like we are flattened to the ground, unable to stand upright and walk. Remember that, similar to the palm tree, God is going to make you stronger through this trial. Your roots of faith in Him are going to dig deeper, and your faith is going to grow greater. You will be able to walk upright once again as you experience the amazing healing that only God can bring to a bereaved parent's heart. Remember that the fruit God can bring out of this will be incredibly sweet. You will be a delight to those around you; a beacon of light and hope to them.

So, take comfort, dear one, from the lesson of the palm tree. Surrender to the Lord in your grief, bend your will to His, and wait with expectation for the sweet fruit that He will bring out of this pain.

"Let your children be as so many flowers, borrowed from God.

If the flowers die or wither, thank God
for a summer loan of them."

—Samuel Rutherford

Chapter 37

In Everything Give Thanks

With Thanksgiving Day coming up and the busyness of the holiday season upon us, fresh emotions surface for those of us who have said goodbye to our little ones. This may be the first holiday year for some of us, and for others, it could be another one. Memories from past years may surface, some of them comforting, yet others that are horrible, causing us to dread this time of year.

As hard as it may be, perhaps we can try to look at the affliction that God has given us to bear with thankfulness. In 1 Thessalonians 5:18, Paul exhorts us, "In everything give thanks: for this is the will of God in Christ Jesus concerning you." You might wish you could sit down beside Paul and say, "Uh, Paul? Did you say to give thanks in *everything*? How can I possibly thank God for having to bury my precious child in the ground? Are you sure about *everything*? Surely you cannot be referring to my situation."

Recently our pastor preached a sermon on this passage, and while I grew up knowing this verse and the ones preceding it, ("Rejoice evermore. Pray without ceasing")—an entirely new perspective washed over me as I heard the sermon. Giving thanks in everything doesn't mean that we are jumping up and down with joy because of our affliction. It doesn't mean we won't feel deep sorrow because of the challenges and devastation that we experience. But we *can* have an inner joy and a grateful heart because God is in control. This didn't happen to us by chance. It was filtered through the loving hands of our Heavenly Father. He has a purpose in it all, and while we don't know that purpose, and would rather not have to experience this, He will not allow this suffering to be useless. He intends to use it for good—both in our lives and in others'.

Giving thanks in all things is not something we always feel like doing. Once again, I am reminded of the lesson that was pressed so hard on me after we lost Serena during labor—*choose to do what is right*. Even when you don't feel like being grateful or thankful, even when you can't see a reason in the world to thank the Lord for the situation you find yourself in, choose to thank Him for Who He is and what He will do with this situation.

Above all of this, please remember to be patient with yourself. It took me a long time to come around to grasping the truths of the lessons the Lord was trying to teach me with the loss of our daughter and the miscarriages that came before and after. This isn't something that happens overnight, or that you acquire in a month or two and move on, happily ever after. The best lessons often take the most time to learn. But what I did find was that every time I made the choice to do what the Lord required and encouraged me to do, even when I didn't feel like it, He blessed me in so many ways. Not to mention it also seemed like a little bit more of my heart was healed in the doing of what He commanded.

Dear one, the Lord is always willing and able to help you. He intercedes for you. He is a merciful and faithful High Priest who was tempted in all points like we are, yet remained sinless. He understands pain. He understands weakness, and He longs for you to bring your broken heart to Him.

So, during this Thanksgiving season, if you don't feel like being thankful, simply pour out your heart to Him. He longs for that intimate fellowship with you. If it's hard to think of words to say, perhaps something like this could help to guide you:

Lord, I know You command me to give thanks in everything, but I am having a terrible time being thankful about my child dying. In fact, I don't even *want* to be thankful. I am angry, hurt, discouraged, and depressed. I know this is not Your will, and I pray that You would grant me the desire to be thankful. Please guard me against the darts of the evil one, who seeks to destroy me with this affliction that You have allowed in my life. You promise that You will work all things together for good to those who love You. Lord, right now, I don't see how any good can come of my devastation.

I honestly don't know how I can thank You for this. Could you please help me to thank You? To see, despite my tears, all of the ways that You have provided for me during this awful time? Could you please help me to be thankful that You have never left my side? Could You please help me to be thankful that this world is not my home and that You have reserved a place in heaven for me? Could You please help me to be thankful for Christ's sacrifice for me and my darling little one so that he/she is now with You? Could You please help me to be thankful that my little one is safe and secure with You, with no temptations, sin or evil to battle with? Please fill my heart with thankfulness so that I may worship You as I ought and give You the sacrifice of praise that You so deserve. Please fill my heart with gratitude so that I may be a beacon of light to those around me.

I would also suggest the song, *Blessings,* by Laura Story as an encouragement. A friend brought this song to my attention a little while after we lost Serena, and it speaks to the fact that we often think of blessings as coming in the form of prosperity, success, family, peace, protection, etc. If we undergo trials, we expect to be delivered from them quickly and expect to heal from pain and suffering.

But what if God's blessings are the things that we don't expect—times of sorrow, sleepless nights, betrayal, storms, and suffering? What if God is actually drawing us nearer to Him and showing us just how much we need Him? What if He is using these challenges to remind us that this world is not our home? What if these trials that we are experiencing are His mercies in disguise? When we can look at our suffering through these lenses—that He intends to bless us in incomprehensible ways—we are able to thank the Lord for the suffering and pain, knowing that He is actually answering our prayers for blessing in a greater way than we could have imagined.

Chapter 38

But We Trusted...

"And, behold, two of them went that same day to a village called
Emmaus, which was from Jerusalem about threescore furlongs.
And they talked together of all these things which had happened.
And it came to pass, that, while they communed together and
reasoned, Jesus Himself drew near, and went with them. But
their eyes were holden that they should not know Him. And He
said unto them, 'What manner of communications are these that
ye have one to another, as ye walk, and are sad?' And the one of
them, whose name was Cleopas, answering said unto Him, 'Art
Thou only a stranger in Jerusalem, and hast not known the things
which are come to pass there in these days? And He said unto them,
'What things?' And they said unto Him, "Concerning Jesus of
Nazareth, which was a prophet mighty in deed and word before
God and all the people: 'And how the chief priests and our rulers
delivered Him to be condemned to death, and have crucified Him.
But we trusted that it had been He which should have redeemed
Israel: and beside all this, today is the third day since these things
were done. Yea, and certain women also of our company made
us astonished, which were early at the sepulchre; And when they

found not His body, they came, saying, that they had also seen
a vision of angels, which said that He was alive. And certain of
them which were with us went to the sepulchre, and found it
even so as the women had said: but Him they saw not.' Then He
said unto them, 'O fools, and slow of heart to believe all that the
prophets have spoken: Ought not Christ to have suffered these
things, and to enter into His glory?' And beginning at Moses and
all the prophets, He expounded unto them in all the scriptures the
things concerning Himself."

—Luke 24:17-27

Can you relate to the two disciples walking on the road? Perhaps you find that you are reasoning with yourself continually, trying to make sense of the tragedy. Perhaps you are reviewing all of the things that you felt were God's signs to you that everything was going to turn out alright. Perhaps you are incredibly confused as to where things went wrong and are trying to figure out how to avoid another situation of devastation in the future. Perhaps you are struggling with communing with the Lord and praying.

The phrase that always stands out to me in this passage is, "**But we trusted that it had been He which should have redeemed Israel…**" They had all of their hopes pinned on Jesus. They had an idea of how they believed God would save Israel and they were counting on Christ to carry out their idea of redemption; their idea of salvation. They had an expectation of how God would work, but it didn't end up happening that way.

It's important to note that they weren't incorrect in their belief; yes, Jesus was the One that would redeem Israel. But it would be in a different way than they anticipated. Rather than treading a path of outward victory and glory, He would go through the valley of the shadow of death, walking a path of shame and humiliation. To the world, He would look like a complete failure. It would appear that the enemy had triumphed. It would look like He was completely powerless. And yet, the outcome was the absolute opposite of what it appeared. Through the pain and suffering, He was actually the victor! He redeemed His people with His own blood that was shed. Satan was defeated, and Christ proved to be the All-Powerful One.

As I think back to those months leading up to Serena's birth and death, I remember the fears and anxieties I had that I would lose her in the womb, especially as I had miscarried Baby Gad prior to her conception. I distinctly remember one night where I felt that I had the assurance of the Lord that everything would be alright. I clung to that assurance, and as the labor and delivery progressed—where everything was going alright—no more thoughts of her loss tormented me. However, at the very end, the Lord saw fit to take her to His arms.

As the days passed after her death, and I tried to make sense of all that had happened, I could relate very well to the disciples in the story above. I had trusted that the Lord would keep her safe—here, in this world. I trusted that I would be able to hold her in my arms and feel the warmth of her living body. I trusted that I would see her eyes focus on me and hear her cries. But instead, He had a different plan. She would be safe and secure in heaven. He would use her to draw me closer to Him, strengthen and deepen my faith, and to cause me to love Him and worship Him just for who He is. He would use her to teach me to learn to do that which is right just because it is right and not because I feel like it, to give me a compassion for others who experience this type of loss and to share the comfort the Lord had granted to me. He would, in fact, make the situation "alright." Just not in the way that I had hoped or imagined.

And so it will be for you! Though the Lord did not answer your prayers as you expected, though His plan for your child was the complete opposite of the one that *you* had, though it seemed like an utter failure and that He was utterly powerless in your situation, remember Christ on the cross. He has already won a great victory for your situation. He is not powerless, and I pray that He will begin, even today, to show you how He will redeem this situation and bring about blessing in your life that you could never have imagined.

Chapter 39

The Man Born Blind for the Glory of God

When we go through a traumatic, devastating situation such as the loss of a child, we are tempted to ask, "Is God angry with me? Is He punishing me for something that I have done?" Our minds try to make sense of the situation and search out a reason for why this tragedy has happened to us.

In recent weeks, I have been studying John 9, and the story of the man who was born blind gives us some refreshing insights into these thoughts.

> *"And as Jesus passed by, He saw a man which was blind from his birth. And His disciples asked Him, saying, 'Master, who did sin, this man, or his parents, that he was born blind?' Jesus answered,* **'Neither hath this man sinned, nor his parents: but that the works of God should be made manifest in him.** *I must work the works of Him that sent Me, while it is day: the night cometh, when no man can work. As long as I am*

in the world, I am the light of the world.' When He had thus spoken, He spat on the ground, and made clay of the spittle, and He anointed the eyes of the blind man with the clay, And said unto him, Go, wash in the pool of Siloam (which is by interpretation, Sent). He went his way therefore, and washed, and came seeing."

—John 9:1-7, emphasis mine

As we can see, the disciples immediately assumed that sin was the reason for this man being blind from birth. How many of us have experienced criticism and judgment from others who voice opinions that assume that we must have done something wrong which caused the death of our child? When you encounter this—and it is highly likely that you will—remember that you are not alone. This blind man (and likely his parents) experienced the same judgment from those around him, including the disciples of Christ.

But notice the love of Christ in this situation: He vindicates the man and sets the record straight. It wasn't because of any particular sin on the part of the man or his parents that this man was born blind. The reason for this affliction was "that the works of God should be made manifest in him." This man was going to be used by the Lord to show the wonderful works that God can, and does, do. His blindness was not by chance, nor was it unknown to the Lord. It was part of God's perfect plan!

Here are a few more "nuggets" gleaned from the Bible Study Fellowship notes that I hope will minister to your heart as they did to mine:

In those days, it was the prevailing teaching that all suffering was a result of either one's sin or their parents' sin.

While Scripture does teach that suffering *can be* a direct result of sin, the Old Testament also clearly teaches that not all suffering is linked to a person's (or their family member's) particular sin. We have seen how the entire book of Job speaks to this truth that those whom God considers as faithful, upright, and righteous experience suffering, and sometimes, it is suffering of the greatest kind. Even though these believers are not able to comprehend the purpose for their suffering, we can know from their lives that God has exalted purposes in their suffering, and none of it is outside of His holy and sovereign care.

It is natural for us to want easy answers when our life is turned upside down by illness, deprivation, betrayal, persecution, or death. Once again, sometimes there are no answers as to why God has allowed pain and sorrow in our lives. While we may not understand, we can know with certainty that God does truly love and care for His children. His greatest demonstration of love was that He sent His Son into the world to live as we live, and ultimately to suffer terribly and die so that we could be saved.

We often think that God is only glorified by miraculous healings. However, the apostle Paul struggled with a "thorn in the flesh"; even though he pleaded with the Lord to remove it three times, God refused to do so. His purpose was to demonstrate to Paul (and to us, thousands of years later) that His grace is sufficient in our weakness. None of us would choose a path of suffering, but there is no greater proof of God's power and grace than that which is seen as He equips His people with a supernatural strength far beyond anything that would come naturally to them. As they remain faithful through devastating circumstances, these children of God experience God's glory in a way that many others know nothing of. So often, this can have an even greater impact than a miraculous healing!

These are the kinds of truths that kept me going in those dark days after Serena died. These truths helped me as I grappled with the questions that filled and plagued my mind. It is my hope and prayer that you, too, will be comforted by the fact that Jesus cares. He will vindicate you. He knows everything and sees the whole picture, and this tragedy in your life is not out of His control or reach. He is going to manifest His glory in a miraculous way—far beyond what you could ever think or imagine! May you rest in the fact that your suffering is not in vain. It has a higher purpose, even when it doesn't make sense.

Chapter 40

Ten-Month Birthday

Dear grieving mother,

Ten months have gone by. I am sure it is easy to try to imagine what your little one would be doing right now—crawling, maybe even starting to stand up while holding on to furniture, getting into everything they can manage, giggling, and interacting with everyone they come in contact with. You may be envisioning gooey fingers and food particles scattered under the high chair as they explore the ever-increasing phenomena of the variety of food options available. They may be still cuddly, or they may be little wiggle worms, wanting to discover and explore the world around them. You long for those interrupted moments, those nights of being awakened, all the laundry from diaper and food messes and whatever inconvenience that parenthood brings if only you could have them in your arms right now. You long to hear their squeals of laughter as you tickle them. You long to see those eyelids close in peaceful, angelic sleep, but it will never be. And you may still be grappling with the "Why?", searching for some Divine revelation as to why your little one was taken away.

In the midst of all that, I would like you to ponder the story of Shadrach, Meshach, and Abednego. We have touched on this story in an earlier chapter, but here, I would like to look at it from a different angle. Just to recapitulate a bit, these were three young Jewish men who had been taken captive from their homeland by Nebuchadnezzar, King of Babylon. They had gained his favor and had been promoted to high positions of honor in the kingdom. One day, King Nebuchadnezzar had a grand idea of making a huge gold image. Once it was sculpted, he commanded that everyone bow down to it when they heard the music begin to play.

However, these three men feared the Lord and would not bow to the image. They were reported and brought to Nebuchadnezzar for questioning. He told them that he would give them another chance, and by bowing down to the image, they would save themselves from being thrown into a fiery furnace. Their response is deeply inspiring: *"Shadrach, Meshach, and Abednego answered and said to the king, 'O Nebuchadnezzar, we are not careful to answer thee in this matter. If it be so, our God whom we serve is able to deliver us from the burning fiery furnace, and He will deliver us out of thine hand, 'O king. But if not, be it known unto thee, 'O king, that we will not serve thy gods, nor worship the golden image which thou hast set up."* (Daniel 3:16-18)

I just love that statement of faith in God's power and their assurance that He could indeed work a miracle on their behalf. Yet, they also acknowledged that God doesn't always work in the way that we want Him to; if He chose not to deliver them, they still would not worship the golden image. Many times, this story from the book of Daniel has bolstered my resolve when I am weakened by grief. I feel like this is one of the precious lessons the Lord taught me through the loss of Serena: He is truly able to do above all that

I ask or think. He *can* work a miracle. But even if He doesn't, I will still praise Him and serve Him only, just like the three Jewish men in the fiery furnace.

Eight years later, after naming Serena's 6th younger sibling, Nathan Azariah (Azariah is the Hebrew name for Abednego), I came across this song by MercyMe, *Even If.* I played this song over and over as tears flowed down my cheeks, thinking back to those first days/weeks after losing Serena and the profound lessons God was now teaching me through her. I would have loved to know about this song when we lost Serena, so I would encourage you to listen to it now if you haven't already. It speaks of how easy it is to praise the Lord and comfort others with God's promises when things are going well. But our faith is really put to the test when a trial hits us, and we are "held to the flame." Our faith is shaken and feels as small as a mustard seed. We know that God can change everything with one word, that He can speak and all the pain will go away, but what if He doesn't? Will we still hope in Him? It is a song of inspiration to cling to Jesus, even in the pain, and I hope that it will encourage and inspire you right where you're at.

Chapter 41

Rejoice for the Glories in Heaven That This World Cannot Offer

It is early in the morning. I have been awake for a couple of hours now, tossing and turning in bed, my mind filled with thoughts as my sister's wedding approaches this weekend. I'm thinking of all of the preparation in store, all of the details to iron out, all of the clothes to pack, all of the items to have in tow; yet, in all of this, my mind goes back to Serena, who would be seven-and-a-half years old now.

She was the child who made my sister an auntie for the first time. She would have been one of the flower girls this weekend. I would have looked for a flower girl dress for her just like I did for our two living daughters. I would have bought the shoes, the hair wreath... the list goes on. I would be packing a suitcase for her, checking off all the items she would need for the exciting trip to Grandpa and Grandma's. I would be mentally figuring out the hairstyle that would suit her best and answering all of her questions as I prepared for the trip. I would be relying on her help with all the last-minute prep just like I rely on Caleb now.

I think back to another sister's wedding nearly six years ago and the yearning in my heart for Serena to be there—to be in the family photos, join us in the celebration, and be a part of all the festivities. A lot has happened since her wedding; a tremendous amount of healing has taken place, and many more lessons have been learned. And yet, the daydreaming of what it would be like if she were here never goes away. That silent ache inside, wishing I could wrap her in my arms and hold her close, never goes away.

I think of the chapter I have been studying this week, John 14, and the rich treasures that I was reminded of in it. Jesus is speaking to His disciples before He would go to His death on the cross, and He says, "Ye have heard how I said unto you, I go away, and come again unto you. If ye loved Me, ye would rejoice, because I said, I go unto the Father: for My Father is greater than I." (John 14:28) We see the disciples in deep sorrow because their greatest and dearest Friend will be leaving them, yet in this time of parting, Christ is encouraging them that the best response is to rejoice. Rejoicing not because they are going to be apart, but because of where He was going and to Whom He was going.

As I think of Serena and how she is with our Father in heaven—how she never knew the guilt and remorse of sin, how she never experienced the consequences for her sin, how she opened her eyes to the glories of heaven, how she has experienced perfect love, peace, and joy, and how she has beheld Jesus—all of the wonderful and exciting things that this world can offer pales in comparison. When I think of the white robe of Christ's righteousness that she is wearing right now, no flower girl dress on this earth can compare to that. When I think of the songs of the angels and the hosts of heaven that she hears, no marriage ceremony can compare to that. When I think of the perfect joy and the freedom from sin she enjoys, no celebration can compare to that.

She knows happiness that I know nothing of. She has a sense of peace and calm that I have never experienced. She knows love's perfection that I don't fully grasp. When my mind turns to this, I am able to say with all honesty, "I can rejoice that she is there, that she is with our Father, that she beholds the face of Christ." When my eyes are turned to this, I understand the peace that only Christ gives that passes all understanding: *"Peace I leave with you, My peace I give unto you: not as the world giveth, give I unto you. Let not your heart be troubled, neither let it be afraid." (John 14:27)*

And so, dear one, it is my hope and prayer that you also will experience the "rejoicing" that Christ encourages us to exercise as you contemplate the wonders that your dear little one is experiencing right now. In that rejoicing, I pray that as your focus is taken off of the temporary pleasures and things that this world offers to the eternal riches and glories that belong to Christ's children, you too can see that everything else truly pales in comparison.

Chapter 42

God Is in Control and Determines the Outcome of Each Story

In the last chapter, I mentioned that I was prepping for a trip to attend my sister's wedding and shared the thoughts and emotions that surfaced regarding our daughter, Serena. The day of the wedding proved to be bittersweet as I met new people and reconnected with old friends, having to navigate the same question over and over: "How many children do you have now?"

Every bereaved parent knows how challenging this question is, and sometimes it is hard to know how to answer. For me, I simply cannot say I only have five children. I feel like I am betraying her if I say that I only have five children and not six. But there is always the follow-up explanation that is needed to clarify that we have five living here and a daughter in heaven (not to mention the three others that were miscarried in the first trimester). Then come the looks of shock or the nods of sympathy. Sometimes a long conversation ensues, while other times, it is brief. While I love talking about her, repeating the same thing over and over on the weekend was a heavier burden than I had anticipated.

Then, on Sunday after the church service, I spoke with a gentleman whose first granddaughter had been born a few weeks earlier. He shared with me a brief summary of how the labor and delivery went, and it sounded much like the labor and delivery that I experienced with our first daughter. Thankfully, this gentleman's granddaughter was born alive, and I sincerely rejoiced in that. But, I have to admit, whenever I hear stories that sound so similar to my birth experience but have ended with a living child, there is a little voice within that still questions, "Why? Why didn't Serena live? Why didn't some miracle happen for her at the end as it did for them?"

Thankfully, I grew up knowing about the sovereignty of God and how everything is in His control. I know that nothing happens out of His plan or without Him allowing it. *"The Lord of hosts hath sworn, saying, 'Surely as I have thought, so shall it come to pass; and as I have purposed, so shall it stand…' For the Lord of hosts hath purposed, and who shall disannul it? And His hand is stretched out, and who shall turn it back?" (Isaiah 14:24, 27)*

But, it was the tragedy and devastation of Serena's death that caused this knowledge of God's sovereignty to make the eighteen-inch journey from my head to my heart. It went from being merely cerebral knowledge to genuinely experiencing the weight and conviction in its fullness. As the months passed after her death and I was faced repeatedly with successful birth experiences, clinging to the truth that God is in control was the only thing that got me through. It was the only thing that helped me truly rejoice for those happy outcomes.

Every birth experience and outcome is sovereignly ordained by His wisdom and loving hands. "...the Lord gave, and the Lord hath taken away; blessed be the name of the Lord." (Job 1:21) While we don't always understand how He could allow our child to die, or how He can bring good out of it, He has proven to me, over and over, that He certainly can.

Oftentimes, there are no human answers that will satisfy our questioning. We simply cannot understand why the three-pound preemie survives, and my nine-pound, two-ounce daughter didn't make it. Why does one twin survive and the other doesn't? Why does one child with a heart defect survive and another doesn't? Why does it seem like a miracle happens for one family and the exact opposite occurs for another?

The world offers us no answers to these questions. It can offer us no real peace or comfort. But standing on the foundation that God is in control, that nothing happens by chance, and that all things are filtered through His loving fingers can give us security when there are no answers. Jesus, the Prince of Peace, offers us comfort in our pain: *"In the world ye shall have tribulation: but be of good cheer, I have overcome the world." (John 16:33)* When we trust that He truly loves us and will cause all things to work for good to those who love Him (Romans 8:28), *"the peace of God, which passeth all understanding, shall keep [our] hearts and minds through Christ Jesus." (Philippians 4:7)*

When the "why's" surface and disturb your peace, may your heart be comforted that God has a perfect plan for you and nothing happens out of His control. He was there every step of the way and will continue to be. He will bring something beautiful out of the devastation that you have experienced. Cling to Him, for as you do, you will know a perfect peace that only He can give.

Chapter 43

Thy Will Be Done

Are you having a hard time surrendering your will to the Lord's? Perhaps in your heart, you know that God allowed these devastating circumstances in your life, and you know that He assures us that He works all things for the good of those who love Him (Romans 8:28). But, do you still find yourself grappling with subjecting your will to the Lord's will? Do you find yourself saying, "Anything, Lord, except my child"? Do you know in your head that you ought to submit to God's will, but deep within there is a raging battle?

Be encouraged, dear mother, that Jesus experienced the same battle within Himself as the time approached for His arrest, trial and crucifixion. In the Garden of Gethsemane, He was in agony, pouring His heart out to His Father. Falling down on His face, He prayed, *"'Father, if Thou be willing, remove this cup from Me: nevertheless, not My will, but Thine, be done.' And there appeared an angel unto Him from heaven, strengthening Him. And being in an agony He prayed more earnestly: and His sweat was as it were great drops of blood falling down to the ground."* (Luke 22:42-44)

The gospels record that He prayed this prayer three times. I especially like Matthew's account of it, where he writes, *"And He said, 'Abba, Father, all things are possible unto Thee; take away this cup from Me: Nevertheless not what I will, but what Thou wilt.'"* Jesus knew that His Father could do anything. *Anything.* Perhaps there could be another way to secure salvation for those whom God had given to Jesus as His inheritance. Perhaps He didn't have to suffer the excruciating pain on the cross, the sting of His Father forsaking Him as He bore the sins of His people, and endure the humiliation from His own countrymen as well as the Romans.

But, no. Death on the cross was the plan set out from before the foundation of the world so that you and I could be saved from the just penalty that we deserved. Even though Jesus wasn't obligated to die on the cross, He *chose* to do so out of love for us as well as love and obedience to His Father. When I consider this, all of the raging waves and storms in my heart quiet. Jesus wasn't thrilled about what He was going to go through. His human nature shrank back from it. But in perfect obedience to His Father, He submitted Himself to the Father's will, and it is because of His submission that my little girl (and my three little miscarried ones) is in heaven right now. Had He decided to say "Not *Thy* will but *Mine* be done," my little girl would be in the torment of hell right now. There would be no hope, comfort, or peace in this life. But instead, there is peace in the pain because Jesus subjected His will to His Father's.

When you feel the battle raging within, follow our Lord's example. Fall down before your heavenly Father in humble prayer. Pour out your heart before Him. Ask Him to help you choose to desire His will above yours, and in so doing, you will learn the blessedness of saying, "Not my will, but Thine be done."

In this past year, as I walked through the loss of my friend's little boy with her, I came across the song *Thy Will Be Done* by Hillary Scott. This song spoke straight to my heart, as it displays the raw pain of what we feel and the reality of the devastation, yet then speaks about submission to the will of the Lord and holding on to the foundational truths that can get us through the heartbreak. This is another song that I wish I knew about when I lost Serena, and I pray that it will be a comfort and encouragement to you today as you grieve for your little one.

Chapter 44

Eleven-Month Birthday

Dear grieving mother,

Just one more month until it will be a year since you said "goodbye" to your little one. Are you feeling apprehensive? Are you dreading it? Do you feel like running away and trying to forget that this awful day ever happened? Are you struggling with how to even treat the day? You may still feel it is the worst day of your life, and are wondering how you could even celebrate. Yet, something within likely tugs at your heart that you really should do something to honor and commemorate your little one.

I remember years where the entire month of July was really tough for me. The first year, I was trying to decide how I would treat the day. I think I was scared about how I would actually feel when it came around. Would I be able to handle it?

I think I was also afraid that no one would say anything or acknowledge our little girl's birthday. My little nephew's 1st birthday was being celebrated at this time, and I made the two-hour trip north to where my in-laws lived. I was alone, as my hubby had a work event. It wasn't easy. I knew that next month no one would be celebrating our little girl's birthday. I didn't know what to expect from family members, and it made me uneasy.

In the years that followed, the month of July continued to be tough for me. I would get an agitated-for-no-reason feeling and stop and think, "What is wrong with me?" Then it dawned on me: *It's July.* There were times I wished her birthday was earlier in the month so that it wouldn't be 28 long days of restlessness, tears, and pain.

Inevitably, the first week would roll around and nearly every day was spent reliving the moments when I was preparing for the arrival of our baby. I remembered those hot afternoons where I would lie down on our bed and relish the movements and gentle pushes of our baby within, knowing that it wouldn't be long before she would arrive and I wouldn't feel those precious movements again. Looking back, I am *so* thankful that I enjoyed those last days of pregnancy.

I can still see myself vacuuming out the vehicle, walking down and back up the huge hill to West Lake Sammamish Parkway, trying to be super fit for the marathon of delivery (and also trying to bring on labor once I was "overdue"). I smile thinking of how our landlord was mortified that I was climbing that hill and said she was sure I would have the baby at the bottom. Oh, if that were the only challenge that it was! I would gladly have taken a short, spontaneous labor with a living baby at the bottom of a hill than the labor that resulted in her exiting this world.

Then, her due date, July 17th, would come and pass. On the day that I had my first contraction with her, I would relive my utter excitement that labor had begun. After that, it was reliving the days and nights I spent laboring to bring her into the world. I had vivid dreams and flashbacks. Being busy with several children didn't always afford time to grieve during the day, so when night fell and I was trying to fall asleep, the waves would hit with the big ugly cry as I tried to silently scream out the pain from the innermost part of my being that still felt like it lodged in my cells. My pillow soaked with tears, I still couldn't make sense of it all. Pleading with Jesus for help and begging Him to soothe my broken heart always helped and gave me the peace I needed to sleep.

It was not until year six or seven that I was able to start looking forward to "celebrating" her birthday and the formal acknowledgment of her life. By that time, I had also come to peace that some family members would never reach out on that day or acknowledge her existence unless I brought it up. The Lord had given me opportunities, over and over again, to learn to be content that all that matters is that *He* remembers and cares. I looked forward to hearing from those family members and friends who *did* remember and who took the time to send me a note or a token of acknowledgment on Serena's birthday.

So, take heart, dear one. The day will come when this time will not be so daunting, foreboding, and gripping. Once again, give yourself time. The decisions you make for this year don't have to be set in stone for years to come. Stay in close fellowship with Jesus as you face this challenging day and know that He will carry you through it.

FOOTPRINTS

One night I dreamed a dream
As I was walking along the beach with my Lord.
Across the dark sky flashed scenes from my life.
For each scene, I noticed two sets
of footprints in the sand,
One belonging to me and one to my Lord.
After the last scene of my life flashed before me,
I looked back at the footprints in the sand.
I noticed that at many times
along the path of my life,
especially at the very lowest and saddest times,
there was only one set of footprints.
This really troubled me, so I
asked the Lord about it.
"Lord, you said once I decided to follow You,
You'd walk with me all the way.
But I noticed that during the saddest and
most troublesome times of my life,
there was only one set of footprints.
I don't understand why, when I needed
You the most, You would leave me."
He whispered, "My precious child, I
love you and will never leave you
Never, ever, during your trials and testings.
When you saw only one set of footprints,
It was then that I carried you."

Chapter 45

Moving from the "Why?" to "What Now?"

Soon after we lost our precious Serena during birth, I remember a close friend saying, "I learned never to question God, and never to ask why." I know they were well-meaning in what they shared, but the idea didn't sit quite right with me. As the weeks and months wore on, I thought on that piece of "advice," and as I submerged myself in the Scriptures to soothe my wounded heart, I discovered why that advice didn't seem quite right. As I read through the Psalms, the Psalmist often questions God:

> *"Why standest Thou afar off, O Lord? Why*
> *hidest Thou Thyself in times of trouble?"*

> —Psalm 10:1

> *"How long wilt Thou forget me, O Lord? For ever?*
> *How long wilt Thou hide Thy face from Me?"*

> —Psalm 13:1

"O God, why hast Thou cast us off for ever? Why
doth Thine anger smoke against the sheep of Thy
pasture? ... Why withdrawest Thou Thy hand, even
Thy right hand? Pluck it out of Thy bosom."

—Psalm 74:1, 10

"Will the Lord cast off for ever? And will He be favorable
no more? Is His mercy clean gone for ever? Doth His
promise fail for ever more? Hath God forgotten to be
gracious? Hath He in anger shut up His tender mercies?

—Psalm 77:8,9

"Lord, why castest Thou off my soul? Why
hidest Thou Thy face from me?"

—Psalm 88:14

Furthermore, as Jesus hung on the cross dying, He Himself asked, "My God, My God, why hast Thou forsaken Me?"

Something I found thought-provoking was the fact that the Psalmist usually didn't end the psalm with the questions he had of God. Rather, he moved from his questions to finding comfort in the truths about God and His character. He moved from despair to hope, from confusion and doubt to purpose, and from uncertainty to faith.

Almost a year later, a book title was mentioned to me, *When Heaven is Silent*. It was written by a pastor, Ron Dunn, whose son had died tragically. Dunn wrote of his experience after that tragedy and the lessons he learned. At that time, it was one of the most comforting and encouraging books I had ever read. It has been several years since I read it, but the message that has stayed with me is this:

"It is normal to ask 'Why?' but we cannot stop there. We need to move on to ask the question, 'What now?'"

The following are a few excerpts from the book that I found great comfort in. I pray that you find the same solace as you read on.

"'Why me?' is a useless question, for in the end, it solves nothing. Only when we face up to the inadequacy of this question will we be free to ask the right one. The *right* question, the one put forth by Christ Himself, is *'what now?'* This question transforms the landscape of suffering from a random, accidental absurdity to a vital part of the grand scheme of a great God."

"The 'why me?' stance afflicts us with tunnel vision, making it impossible to see anything but the 'unfairness' of our predicament. 'It imprisons one within the chaos.'"

"But 'what now?' allows us to step outside that prison and see ourselves not as hapless victims but as objects of divine attention..."

"'What now?' breaks the trance of self-pity..."

"When we ask 'What now?' we shift our focus from ourselves to God and what He is up to in our lives. And He is up to something. But we will never see it with our eyes turned selfward. If we can say to our adversities what Joseph said to his brothers—'And as for you, you meant evil against me, but God meant it for good (Gen 50:20)—we will gain a fresh, confident and creative direction in life. God does not give an answer to every 'Why?' but He gives assurance to every 'who.'"

"Not only does 'What now?' save us from self-pity, but it also gives us something to look forward to. 'What now?' means we are still moving, still growing. In short, we have a future. It means that life can be good again."

"When through the settling dust of collapsed hopes we can ask, 'What now?' we are testifying to a faith that believes God saves the best until last."

"Finally, asking 'What now?' makes us a part of God's work." (PP.90-96)

It is my hope that as you grapple with the questions which arise in your heart and mind during this time, the Lord will help you to look beyond the "Why?" to the "What now?" looking forward with great expectation to see what He has in store for you. May He grant you eyes to see how He can transform this tragedy into something far beyond your imagination.

Chapter 46

Promises from the Prince of Peace

Are you feeling like all you need is just a dose of peace? If you could only quiet the aching in your heart and the questions and doubts that pop up at random times; if only you could feel a peace washing over your soul as the streams of water running along in a brook... That would be like heaven! From my experience, clinging to the promises of Christ and the peace that He gives helped me through the days I thought I couldn't make it through. His words afford much greater comfort than the words of any friend or confidant. I pray that your heart will be filled with the following words from the Prince of Peace and that you find comfort in His arms of love every moment of every day.

> *"Thou wilt keep him in perfect peace, whose mind is stayed on Thee: because he trusteth in Thee. Trust ye in the Lord for ever: for in the Lord JEHOVAH is everlasting strength."*
>
> —Isaiah 26:3,4

"He healeth the broken in heart, and
bindeth up their wounds."

—Psalm 147:3

"I will not leave you comfortless; I will come to you."

—John 14:18

"These things I have spoken unto you that in Me ye
might have peace. In the world ye shall have tribulation:
but be of good cheer: I have overcome the world."

—John 16:33

"For Thou has been a strength to the poor, a strength
to the needy in his distress, a refuge from the storm,
a shadow from the heat, when the blast of the
terrible ones is as a storm against the wall."

—Isaiah 25:4

"He giveth power to the faint; and to them that have no
might He increaseth strength. Even the youths shall faint
and be weary, and the young men shall utterly fall: But
they that wait upon the Lord shall renew their strength;
they shall mount up with wings as eagles; they shall run,
and not be weary, and they shall walk and not faint."

—Isaiah 40:29-31

"… Fear not: for I have redeemed thee, I have called thee
by thy name; thou art Mine. When thou passest through the
waters, I will be with thee; and through the rivers, they shall
not overflow thee: when thou walkest through the fire, thou
shalt not be burned; neither shall the flame kindle upon thee."

—Isaiah 43:1-2

"When a child is born, it is the mother's
instinct to protect the baby.

When a child dies, it is the mother's
instinct to protect the memory."

—Unknown

Chapter 47

Finding the Blessing in Painful Anniversaries

As I pondered what to write this week, I found myself thinking of all of the little ones whose anniversaries just passed or who are coming up in a couple of weeks: Gabriella Grigoryevnna' s 8th anniversary on April 12th, Brynn Ruth's 1st anniversary on April 17th, Isabella Joy's 4th on April 25th, Judah Daniel's 3rd anniversary coming up on May 4th, Ella Marie's 7th on May 5th and Britton Ione's 3rd on May 7th.

The days leading up to these anniversaries are very tough. Even though our Serena went to be with Christ during birth nearly eight years ago, I always find the month of July to be more emotional than usual. I have found that as time passes, the sting lessens and the aches aren't as overwhelming. Still, there is the same struggle of wishing we could erase the loss of our child and not have to face it year after year, but still holding on to that day as it validates that which our heart and mind will never let us forget—we *have* another child.

As I spoke with one of the moms whose little girl's anniversary is coming up soon, she spoke of the pain that she is experiencing along with all the memories that flashback at the strangest and most unexpected of times. I encouraged her that I try to embrace all of the memories that surface at this time as a blessing—something that God gives to us to validate the fact that we have another child. Even though that little one is gone, our hearts and minds are still connected to that child, and no matter how much time passes, nothing will erase the reality that we have them as part of our family and that he or she is waiting for us in heaven.

When we can focus on the anniversary of their death as something that can actually bless us, it can be a tremendous step in the healing process. It doesn't mean that there will be no more tears. It doesn't mean that you won't experience all of those questions and thoughts that may surface as you remember the circumstances of your child's death. But looking at it through the lens that God is giving you a special time to celebrate that child who is no longer here can become a blessing to you that you would have never imagined.

I would encourage you to think ahead (before your child's anniversary is upon you) and decide what you envision would be a joyful and special way to remember your little one. Ponder how you can celebrate the time that you did have with him or her. Some ideas you might want to consider to commemorate your little one include:

- Visiting and decorating the gravestone.

- Making a special dinner that focuses on favorite foods you enjoyed during your pregnancy with that child.

- Writing your memories on slips of paper and putting them in a bottle. The following year, you could open the bottle and read those messages together as a family.

- Creating a scrapbook of photos, memories, and memorabilia.

- Making memory bracelets or stones.

- Visiting a special place that holds memories for you.

- Sharing memories with others.

For our family, we always take all of our children to the cemetery, lay flowers on Serena's grave, and take a family photo. Then, we enjoy Jamba Juice smoothies as it is usually a hot summer day and they are extra refreshing! I also write a post on social media (or send it in e-mail form to friends and family that would appreciate it) that is intended to acknowledge her and speak of the mercy and grace of Christ to encourage others in their struggles. I bake a cake (often with the children's help) and decorate it.

In the first few years after her death, I included something in the cake decoration that spoke to a particular lesson I had learned that year in the healing process. In the evening, we often watch the slideshow of the (not-enough) photos that we have of her and her burial, which always results in tears flowing down my cheeks. But through it all, I feel the peace of the Lord underlying everything, and He gives grace to enjoy the fact that we *can* remember her and celebrate her as being part of our family.

I hope that this will encourage you to embrace this difficult day and the equally tough days leading up to it as a blessing that God has given to you. Though the pain will be more intense at first, it will likely lessen as the years go by. Depending on what is going on in your life at the time, some anniversaries may be tougher than others, but I would encourage you to find things that can help you focus on the special memories and the hope you have. May the Lord bring a smile to your face despite the tears that may flow.

Chapter 48

1st Birthday

Dear grieving mother,

Today is the day. Today is the day that shattered your world and broke your heart into uncountable pieces.

How are you doing? How are you feeling?

In some ways, it may not seem like a whole year has gone by. You have learned that you can live without your precious little one, even though at one time you never could have dreamt that was a remote possibility. In other ways, it might seem like forever since you held your precious little one. The ache and longing to hold them just one more time, to kiss their cheeks and see them look into your eyes can be overwhelming, and you may find yourself still drowning in grief.

I remember Serena's 1st birthday well. I was seven-and-a-half months pregnant with Caleb, and we had a friend from Hungary staying with us who was also working for my husband. I remember the tears flowing as I baked her birthday cake and having to explain my out-of-sorts state to our guest. We stopped by my husband's office before we went to the cemetery as I needed to laminate the decorative topping I made to place on top of her cake. The secretary, Rene, who was also a good friend of mine, came around the desk and squeezed me tightly, whispering a prayer in my ear, asking the Lord to comfort my heart that day. We both wiped away tears, and I left with a sweet memory I will never forget.

My husband and I picked up flowers and drove over to the cemetery in Seattle. We walked across the lawn, reliving the memories of the previous year. We stood there side by side, arms around each other, in silence. I didn't know how my husband would handle it. He hadn't been keen on accompanying me to the cemetery but had agreed to go when he saw how distressed I was that he wasn't planning on doing so. We laid the flowers on her gravestone and took photos. Then, we went out to eat at Chipotle and had Jamba Juice smoothies. We both remembered how intense the heat was the previous year. I don't remember what we did for the rest of the day, but we ate the cake I had baked and decorated. Once the day was over, it felt like a relief. I had made it through.

Perhaps it is the same for you. Perhaps you are just waiting for this day to pass. Perhaps you are encouraged that you made it through. Perhaps you have some sweet memories from this day as others may have remembered that it was the anniversary of your little one's departure. On the other hand, it could have been extra painful if no one remembered or acknowledged this monumental day in your life.

I pray that the Lord gives (and gave) you the strength and the grace to face this day—to take the time to cry and grieve, yet to grieve with hope, knowing that your child is with Him in glory, free from all pain and suffering and enjoying the glories and perfection of heaven. May He bless you with the special memories you have of your little one while they were here with you on the earth, no matter how brief it may have been. May He give you the grace to continue to cling to Him and proceed with the journey.

Chapter 49

Ways that Family and Friends Can Help Grieving Parents (Words)

Often, when the death of a child occurs, more hurt is inflicted, or the burden of suffering is heightened by the response of family members and friends. It isn't that they are trying to be unkind, hurtful, or insensitive. Chances are, they haven't experienced this kind of devastation and are simply unsure of how to respond or what to say. There's a chance they might be experiencing their own share of grief and aren't able to be very supportive because of it.

I want to spend the bulk of this chapter sharing some thoughts from my own (and others') experience of how friends and family members can be supportive. We'll move in two sections, first focusing on the words and phrases that can come across as hurtful, and then what can be said to minister healing instead. If you find that it may be helpful to share with friends and family so they can understand how to best support you during this time of grief, please do so.

1. **"At least you are young; you can have more children."**

   Being young doesn't minimize the pain that a parent feels when they lose a child. No subsequent pregnancy or child can ever replace the one that was lost.

2. **"Be thankful for the children that you have."**

   Though I have been blessed with six living children after Serena and experienced two miscarriages after her, none of those pregnancies could ever replace her. I'm still aware of the "spot" where she would be standing or sitting every time we take a family photo. I still have days where I feel like I am missing a child, but when I do a headcount, all of the living children are there. No child can replace another.

3. **"It was God's will."**

   As Christians, we know that nothing occurs outside of the will of God. But sometimes, doctrine and theology are not very helpful when hearts are bleeding. When Jesus spoke with Martha and Mary after the loss of Lazarus, He knew that Lazarus' death was for the glory of God. However, He didn't say that to Martha and Mary right when they came out to Him, stricken with grief, saying, "If you had been here, Lord, we know our brother would not have died." Instead, He pointed Martha to the hope of the resurrection and His identity as the resurrection and the life. Let's not forget the magnitude of how He wept along with them, even though He knew He would be raising Lazarus from the dead within the next hour.

4. **"Everything happens for a reason."**

   Much like the "It's God's will" statement, though it is true that God is in control of everything and allows certain things to happen in our lives that we cannot understand, it just isn't helpful in the moment. In fact, the timing and context of this comment may do more ill than good for a grieving parent.

5. **"God only gives you what you can handle."**

A grieving parent will likely feel as if they can't handle this statement. They may be feeling like they are barely hanging on to begin with. Once again, be careful when bringing doctrine and theology into your conversation. There is a time and place for it, but sometimes a parent just needs a listening ear or compassionate heart rather than sound theological statements.

6. **"The child may have been handicapped."**

I found this comment to be enraging. As if I would rather have a dead child than a handicapped child?! I wanted to scream, "Who are you to say whether my child would have been handicapped or not? I would have loved that child just as much as if they were handicapped! God will give the grace to handle a handicapped child if it is His will!"

7. **"It is time to get over it and move on."**

As a bereaved mother, I don't feel like one ever really "gets over" the loss of a child. When a death is unexpected and sudden, I think it may take even longer to grieve, simply because there was no time to even begin to process anything. There was no time to prepare, no time for goodbyes, no time to "get things in order." Regardless of whether the death was unexpected or expected, "getting over it" doesn't seem like a reality. While as time goes by, the sting lessens and the anguish diminishes, there will always be a "hole" in your heart. I like to say it this way: "There will always be a hole in your heart; but in time, a bridge is built over it." Or, "The wound will heal, but the scar will always remain." Grief takes time; there are forward steps and then some backward steps too. The best thing you can do to support a grieving parent is to be there on both the good days and the tough days.

8. **"They are in a better place."**

Yes, for those of us who know the Lord, our little ones are with Him in heaven. It is the best place that they can ever be. However, that doesn't take away the feeling of being robbed of the time that we had expected they would be here with us (especially based on the natural order where children should outlive their parents). It doesn't take away the fact that our hearts are bleeding. There is a time to point the grieving parent to the hope that we have in heaven, but be careful about how and when you do it. Try to be cautious that you don't minimize the pain by pointing them to doctrine.

9. **"At least we know where they are."**

Once again, I understand that grieving parents who are Christians don't have to grieve without hope, for they know that their little ones are with the Lord. But please be sensitive to the situation. Someone once told me, "At least we know that she is in heaven rather than being kidnapped or raped." This was something that I reminded myself of when I was having difficulty cultivating an attitude of gratitude as I dealt with the grief of her absence. However, depending on the timing of this comment and the context of the conversation, it could really hurt a grieving parent. Be careful when trying to convey hope to parents as sometimes, all that they need is for you to listen and let them cry.

10. **"Have faith."**

To be honest, when one goes through the loss of a child, it can be incredibly faith-rocking. I am thankful that the Lord holds on to those who are His because if it were not for Him, I would have never made it through the loss of Serena. Looking back, I know He held my hand tightly when I was too weak to hold on. He loved me through all of the questions, doubts, and rollercoaster of emotions. He was tremendously patient with me as I learned important lessons that didn't come so quickly. "Having faith" doesn't keep one from experiencing some of the most awful tragedies of life. "Having faith" doesn't mean that you can get through those awful tragedies on your own. I believe God is the One who gives us the faith to keep holding on to Him, and when we come out stronger on the other side, to God be the glory!

11. **"Don't ask God 'why' and don't question Him."**

I have already written about this in an earlier chapter, but I think that there is ample testimony in the Scriptures that it is okay to ask God "Why?" and question Him about your circumstances. Even Christ on the cross said, "My God, My God, why hast Thou forsaken Me?" However, moving beyond the "Why?" to "What next, Lord? What would You have me to do with this situation?" is important in the healing process.

12. **"At least you had (X) amount of time with them."**

I understand that the "at least" statements are meant to help parents focus on what they can be thankful for rather than the pain of the situation. While that can be helpful in raising them out of the spiral of depression, it can also be very hurtful. Serena died during labor and delivery, and I had *no* time with her outside of the womb. I have no memories to look back on and am unable to cherish all of the things that she did outside of the womb. I never saw her look into my eyes. I never saw her smile. I never heard her call me "Mama." Some people have said that it was better that she died young—before I had all of those memories to cause me more pain. I, on the other hand, wish I had more memories with her to hold on to. Either way, when a child has died, there is *never enough* time that you could have had with them. Once again, be careful when saying things that are true but might not be helpful at the time.

13. **"I am so happy to see you are a mother of _____ children."** **(not including the one that is deceased)**

This past Mother's Day, a friend of mine sent me a text saying, "I am so happy to see you as a mother of five children!" To be honest, I would rather not receive a Mother's Day greeting if Serena isn't going to be included in the count of my children. I personally understand if people don't want to include the three first-trimester miscarriages I have had, making me a mother of ten, but could you please include my full-term child who was held in arms by family members and has a plot in the cemetery with a gravestone marking? Or simply don't mention the number of children I have if you can't bear to include my deceased daughter. For those who have had a miscarriage(s), I believe it is special that you include those little ones in the count. Think of it this way: if they had only had miscarriages and no living children, would you not say anything about them being parents? Just because they have no living children to "show-case," does that disqualify them from being a parent?

14. **Don't compare your loss of a spouse, sibling, grandparent, parent, coworker, pet, etc. to the loss of a child**.

    Everyone's loss is different. Everyone grieves differently, and the loss of a child is much different than other losses. Draw from the experience that you have in dealing with grief to support them, but please don't compare.

15. **Don't say "I know your pain," especially when you haven't lost a child or a loved one**.

    This goes along with #14. When people try to act like they know how a grieving parent is feeling, it doesn't go too well. Grieving parents need understanding, support, and care rather than someone to attempt to "fix" the devastation they are feeling.

I am sure that there are many more platitudes that I haven't mentioned, each one being equally hurtful, but the main idea is to please be sure that you are thinking through what the grieving parents might be feeling and don't speak without first thinking it through.

Now that we have talked about the things that are not helpful to say, let's cover a few things that could be helpful to someone who is grieving the loss of a child.

1. **Show empathy.**

    If you don't know what to say, then simply say nothing at all; just be a listening ear.

2. **Stick with the simple.**

   The following are some simple phrases that mean the world to a parent's hurting heart:

   "I am so sorry."

   "I can't imagine what you are going through."

   "I am praying for you."

   "How can I help you?"

   "This hurts."

   "I love you."

   "I am here."

3. **"Tell me about him/her."**

   Often, people shy away from talking about the deceased child because they are afraid that bringing up the subject will only cause a fresh fountain of tears and hurt the parent even more. From my personal experience, talking about Serena, while it may bring tears, is tremendously therapeutic. It brings me joy and peace to speak about her and talk about the few memories I have to share of her pregnancy, labor, and delivery. Rather than having to keep it all inside, it is wonderful to be able to share it with someone. Having someone ask me to share about it is a blessing I can't put into words. It shows that they care enough to bring it up and to listen.

   On the other hand, I understand that for some parents, it is too painful and they don't wish to talk about it. I would recommend that you carefully broach the subject, saying something like, "I just want you to know that if you would like to talk about your child, I would love to hear about him/her. I want to be here to support you and help you, so if it would, please know that I am happy to listen."

4. **Talk about the memories you have of their child and share stories of what you remember.**

Depending on how long the pregnancy lasted or how long the child lived, the memories and stories will reflect that. But if there is absolutely *anything* that you can share about the joy their child brought to your heart or how special they were to you, share it. It will be an incredible blessing.

5. **Always include that child whenever you talk about how many children they have.**

When I was expecting our 6th child, I saw a friend who I hadn't seen for years, and she said to me, "So you are working on number six?" I can't tell you how wonderful it was to hear that. Most people would have said "number five," but she knew that we had lost Serena seven years earlier. It meant so much to me to hear her, on her own accord, include Serena in the count of children, especially when I feel like I often have to explain how many children I do have.

6. **Encourage them.**

Similar to #2, the following encouragements are like water to a grieving parent's soul:

"This is so tough, but I know you will make it through."

"You are being so strong."

"Today is a tough day, but you aren't a failure."

"This is totally contrary to nature—we never expect to bury our children—but you are doing an amazing job in this horrible situation."

"Jesus is holding onto you."

"God is carrying you."

"Even if it feels like He isn't there, keep clinging tightly to Him."

"If you feel like you are slipping, Jesus is going to catch you."

"You will smile again."

"You will see the light at the end of this awfully dark tunnel."

7. **If you have experienced the loss of a child, share your experience in a manner that will give them hope that they *will* get through this.**

   I probably don't really need to write this because I have found that oftentimes when people have gone through a loss and come through, they want to reach out to others because they understand how enormously deep the pain is. But in case you *are* holding back from sharing your story, please be encouraged to reach out. When the few women shared their losses with me (some that had happened 15-20 years earlier) and I saw them now living vibrant, fruitful lives, I was given hope that I would make it through and come out on the other side.

While I am sure that much more could be added to these lists from the experiences of others, it is my hope that these thoughts from my own experience can help friends and family members support grieving parents by way of words.

Chapter 50

Ways that Friends and Family Can Hurt or Help Grieving Parents (Actions)

In the last chapter, we looked at the words that family and friends can say to either increase or alleviate the pain. In this chapter, let's focus on *actions* that friends and family can utilize to support those grappling with the loss of their precious child.

1. **Attend the funeral or memorial service of the child.**

    This demonstrates to the parents how much you care about their lost child, and that you desire to be there to support them during this devastating time.

2. **Remember that your help and support will be needed long-term.**

    It often takes three to four years to get over an expected death, and five to six years for an unexpected death. If that is correct, then this is the beginning of a very long journey with many ups and downs. Fresh waves of grief are going to roll in on the anniversaries, family celebrations and events, graduations, weddings, the birth of other children, holidays, subsequent deaths of loved ones, etc. When someone understands this and is willing to be there through every up and down, this is incredibly touching to a grieving parent, even though they may not initially express this to you.

3. **Think practically.**

   Grieving parents need space to process. Many times, it is a challenge just to get out of bed in the morning. Many parents don't feel like eating or proceeding with basic things like cooking and cleaning. If you want to help, provide meals, offer to keep up the garden/yard, clean the house, and run errands for them. At this time, depending on the situation, there are a host of decisions they have to make regarding burial plans and everything else surrounding the life of their child. Shouldering some of the mundane things is a huge blessing to them, no matter how insignificant it may seem.

4. **Be there.**

Let them know that you are there for them, whether they are crying, screaming, or just needing silence and space. Sometimes, they will ask to be alone, and that needs to be honored. But remember that doesn't mean they necessarily want to be alone forever, just maybe for that specific time. They are likely still trying to process the situation and all the repercussions that come from it, and their emotions are going to be all over the place. Whether or not they take you up on your offer, it is still heartwarming to hear the words, "I'm here for you."

5. **Be prepared to give a lot of grace and unconditional love**.

   As just mentioned, parents' emotions are on a rollercoaster as they are trying to adjust to the "new normal." There may be times where they snap at you or say hurtful things in response to the kindness you have shown. Remember that they are likely not angry with you; they are just trying to deal with the pain.

6. **Don't expect much from the parents, especially in the first few months**.

   Life is *never* going to be the same for them again. In the first weeks, months and years depending on the person, they will never wake up without thinking about that child. They are going to replay every detail, second-guess decisions, and are going to be tempted to blame. They may not want to leave their house or see anyone. They may struggle with depression and anxiety, nightmares and times where they are lost in their thoughts, not really being tuned in to their surroundings. There will never be a day where they won't have at least a little tug in their subconscious that their child is not here. No matter how much peace they find as the journey progresses, their life will never be the same. The things they used to find joy in may no longer be the same. They may begin to devote a part of their life to ministering to others who also experience the same pain, or they may begin doing something in memory or honor of their child. Some may never be able to do certain activities or go to certain places without breaking down because of the memories it holds. Think of it like a broken bone. While healing does occur, that bone is never the same again.

7. **Pray for them**.

Even if they ask you to stop praying for them, continue to do so in private. Often, parents' faith is shaken, and they can't understand why God allowed this to happen. Sometimes they wonder why a miracle didn't happen for them as it happened for others. They need your prayers as often they may feel too weak and wounded to pray for themselves.

8. **Remember and acknowledge their loss**.

Speaking from personal experience, it was those few people who took the time over the past eight years since Serena died to mention her or acknowledge her that really soothed my wounded Mama heart. Recalling that I do have another child, or remembering that our first daughter born after her, Nadine, was given her middle name were little things that meant so much.

Here are a few ideas of how to acknowledge and remember in a healing way:

* Send a note every month on the anniversary of the child's passing.

* Send a note on the first anniversary: this one is usually the hardest, and parents need your support.

* But don't stop after a year! Every year, send a note remembering the day that is a sorrow to them.

* Send a note on Mother's Day and Father's Day, acknowledging that they are the parent of another child, even though he/she is not here. Hearing from you will help ease the burden.

* You may also consider getting something special for the parents or the siblings on the anniversary of the child's death or the child's birthday. Make a cake on the birthday and take it over.

* Send flowers.

For the rest of their lives, these parents will carry the loss in their hearts. When you send a card, drop a note, make a phone call, or do something special, you are helping to shoulder that burden.

9. **Say the name of the child.**

Sometimes, it seems that people are afraid to speak of the deceased child. They feel that it might make the pain harder on the parents. On the contrary, from my own personal experience, when someone speaks of Serena on their own initiative, while I may get some tears in my eyes, it is not because they have reminded me of her. I never forget her. However, the tears are often because someone cared enough to remember her and bring it up.

10. **Accept that the parents will never be the same again.**

Similar to #6, the death of a child causes great change in the lives of their family. It may be hard to accept this, but it will be a relief to the parents that you don't expect them to be the same as they were before this tragedy. They may be struggling with the fact that they are not the same and they wish that they could be. Your supportive attitude will help them learn to accept their new identity, as they will always carry the scars of the loss of their child and pleasures, hobbies, and pastimes may not look the same anymore. They will have to learn to smile and laugh again. They will have to find joy again in a life where there are constant reminders that their child is not there with them.

11. **Visit the cemetery.**

You have no idea how much it means to parents that you have taken the time out of your life and activities to respect the memory of their child. Let them know that you stopped by. Leave a note or flowers at the cemetery. Again, from personal experience, when my sister-in-law came with me to the cemetery after the gravestone was placed, it meant a lot to me. On the other hand, it hurts that other family members have never taken the time to visit the cemetery.

12. **Don't be afraid of their tears.**

Let them know that with you, they have a "safe" place to cry. Sometimes, people get very uncomfortable and don't want to witness tears and weeping. They can't handle sorrow and pain. This causes the parents additional anxiety and causes them to want to withdraw from social interactions. If you offer a reassuring hand on their shoulder as they cry, or a tissue, and are willing to listen to them as they speak through their tears, it will help them as they release the pent-up emotion within.

13. **Be willing to just sit and listen, even if they say the same things over and over again.**

It is all a part of processing the intense grief that they are experiencing. They are trying to make sense of the awful pain, and their mind is in a constant state of analyzing, reliving everything that led up to the tragedy, trying to figure out how they could have ensured a different outcome, etc. They aren't getting a rest from the doubts, and perhaps guilt-trips are starting to plague their mind. They may be trying to justify to themselves how they are not responsible for this tragedy, and they want to ensure that everyone else knows they aren't to blame either—that they did what they knew best, and that they made the best decisions with the information and experience that they had. While you can talk to them and get them into a better frame of mind, within the next hour, they could be right back to the previous state. Basically, their mind has to be re-programmed as they accept the fact that their worst nightmare has become their reality. Be patient with them. As time goes on, and they adjust, the repetition will go away.

14. **Try not to judge**.

Grieving parents may do things that you are not totally comfortable with. They may wear a T-shirt with the child's picture. They may visit the grave every day, or twice a day. They may plaster the walls with photos of the child. They may dedicate a room to hold all of the mementos that they have of the child (remember, this is all that they have left now). They may even have some inaccurate theological views on what the child is doing in heaven now. Whatever the case is, please consider that this may not be the time to talk to them about it. Unless it is something harmful to them or others, simply give them time and space to work through the grief.

15. **Make or purchase a special gift to commemorate their child that they can treasure.**

    This speaks volumes to parents. The fact that you spent the time to think about, create, or purchase something significant and special to acknowledge and remember their child is a tremendous blessing that you will never completely understand. Perhaps you buy a potted plant so that every time that plant blooms, they can remember you were thinking of their child. Plant a tree in their memory. Buy or make a piece of jewelry that they can wear, a stitchery, a personalized teddy bear, blanket, painting, quilt, collage... the list goes on and on.

    I can't tell you how wonderful it was when I opened up a framed stitchery done by a family friend with Serena's photo, name, and birthdate on it. It hangs on our dining room wall with all the other birth announcements that she has done for our subsequent children. To know that she cared enough to include our deceased daughter is a feeling I can never describe. I feel like I can't thank her enough.

16. **Watch for signs that they may need professional help.**

    Experiencing the loss of a child is a pain that pierces the very core of one's inner being, and there are some who cannot move beyond their pain. Be on alert for behavior that is dangerous to themselves or to others. Don't panic but help them search out a support group. Offer to go along with them.

17. **Help with surviving siblings.**

    I feel like I can't offer a lot of advice in this area because we experienced our loss when we didn't have any other children. However, I do know that dealing with the demands, needs, and grief of the remaining children can be very exhausting without adding the oppressive burden of your own grief. Consider taking the sibling(s) to a park or another energy-intensive outing. Invite the children over to bake cookies, do an art project or craft. Just remember that the siblings are dealing with their own grief after losing their sibling and they need to be supported as well.

18. **Set a regular time that they can count on you to offer tangible support.**

Perhaps this looks like coming by every Friday afternoon to help with the laundry, or Saturday morning to help clean the house. If there are other children, perhaps it is every Tuesday at 4 pm to take the children out to the park. Maybe it looks like offering to take the children to their weekly dance/piano/art lessons or soccer/baseball practice.

Oftentimes, after the death of a child, parents find it hard to go out. First, they have to deal with the questions and the immense grief. Then there are the tears that pour out at some of the most unusual and inopportune times. Helping them ease back into being out in the world in any way possible is a huge help.

19. **Be careful in expressing your excitement in the achievements of your children, or a new pregnancy or birth.**

While you need to celebrate these important things in your family's life, be aware that these things may be like salt in your friend's open wounds. I remember the stinging pain I felt when an old penpal of mine gave birth to a baby girl three weeks after we lost Serena. I remember when one of my husband's employees announced she was expecting, and "It is a girl!" came out of her mouth. I knew it was right to be happy for them, so I prayed for grace to rejoice, but it was not easy. Share your intense excitement with friends or family who are not grieving, and "tone it down" for those who have just experienced loss. Wait to share that you are expecting another baby if they just lost theirs. Wait to share about your child's accomplishment if they were in the same class as the child who is no longer living. Guard what you say and do so out of love for those who are hurting deeply right now.

20. **Consider a monetary gift.**

Losing a child is a big enough burden to carry by itself. Adding (sometimes astronomical) hospital bills, funeral, burial and gravestone expenses can be overwhelming to parents. I remember the immense burden it was when the hospital and doctor bills started coming in after Serena's death. It was one thing to pay those bills and have a living child in your arms, but it was quite another to be paying those bills when she was *not* here. Receiving a monetary gift from a widow who had also just lost her son, as well as a monetary gift from my parents, was a tremendous blessing to us as it helped to alleviate the financial burden during that devastating time.

21. **Find support for yourself as well.**

Supporting someone through the process of grief is not easy. There may be misunderstandings. At times, you may feel like you are ignored or that your actions of love are unappreciated. Your friend will likely be finding it very hard to maintain their part of the relationship as they grapple with the life-changing event of the death of their child. Remember that they are not trying to hurt you. They simply can't manage both. But, they do need you; regardless of how they may respond at times. So, don't give up on them. Just be sure to find people that can fill the needs you have so you can continue to support your friend.

I am certain that other bereaved parents could add so much more about what would be helpful and supportive to them, but I hope that these ideas can be a starting point to assist friends and family in knowing how they can help when they may feel at a loss as to what they can do. It is my hope that being aware of these things will help to minimize the hurt that bereaved parents often experience simply because friends and family don't know how to help.

Chapter 51

The Journey Continues...

A few months ago, a family visited our church with four children in tow. Their eldest daughter was seven-years-old, and her eighth birthday is actually today. As we drove home, it struck me: she is the same age Serena would be right now. As I thought about how grown up that young girl is, I can't believe so much time has gone by. At the same time, so much has occurred in the past eight years that often it seems like all that happened is merely a memory.

When I think back to those days and nights after we lost Serena, remembering the horrific ache and pain that I felt, I wouldn't have imagined my life as it is now. I now have five living children and another little one on the way.

Back then, everything looked dismal and dreary. I felt hopeless; in deep despair. I wondered if I would ever have any living children after a miscarriage, stillbirth, and another miscarriage. But praise be to the Lord! He has turned my mourning into dancing. He has given me blessings that I don't deserve. He has taught me so much through the loss of our daughter and the little ones I miscarried in the 1st trimester. And best of all, their death isn't the end of the story—it is just the beginning!

I want to encourage you, dear grieving one, that the same can happen to you as well. You will smile again. You will find joy in life again. Yes, you are a changed person, and you will never be the same from here on out. You will always bear the marks of the child that you no longer hold in your arms here. You will carry their memory in your heart forever.

But I want to encourage you to step out and see what special thing the Lord would have you do now. Take it day by day. Some of the things He may ask you to do will be hard, like reaching out to a family that has a living child the same age as yours and doing something special with them- as difficult as that may be. The Lord will bless your efforts to take the painful situation He allowed in your life to bring joy and life to others.

I also want to encourage you to beseech Him for love, forgiveness, gentleness, and kindness to those around you who don't truly understand what you have been through (and what you continue to go through). It has been eight years for me, and those lessons didn't come overnight. It was a long journey of learning to forgive those who unintentionally hurt because they simply did not (and could not) understand. They had never experienced the loss of a child. They had different views on life in the womb and stillbirth. They wanted to have "answers." They couldn't get beyond a "perfect" world and accept that this was my reality.

But year after year, the Lord brought situations over and over again to help me learn to release that pain to Him. He taught me how to choose to love and forgive rather than dig my heels in the ground and "make them pay for their insensitivity." He gave me the courage to decide that a relationship with others was more important than my right to grief and my needs in grief.

Developing and nurturing a deeper understanding that God cares, knows, and understands was SO instrumental in helping me to let go and cast my burdens on Him. I haven't learned these lessons perfectly. I still have a lot of growing to do, and when certain situations arise, I have to make a conscious choice to either hold onto the grudge or forgive, but I am so grateful that the Lord is patient with me and helps me along this rocky path.

I just want to encourage you through all of this that the Lord is patient with you too. It may *feel* like you can never forgive or love, but you can still choose to do so. Ask Him to help you, and He **will** answer that prayer, for it is in accordance with His will for us. At first, it may seem like things get worse as He brings more opportunities (i.e., more hurt) to forgive into your life. But in the end, you will come forth as shining gold that will reflect more of Christ's image to all of those around you.

Take heart, dear grieving one. The Lord is by your side. He will never leave you nor forsake you. He walks in this dark valley with you, and you *will* come out on the other side!

Chapter 52

Always Loved, Never Forgotten

> *"Some say you are too painful to remember.*
>
> *I say you are too precious to forget."*
>
> —Unknown

As I come to the completion of this book with hopes of publishing it on the 10th anniversary of our precious little girl's birthday, I want to share some of the memoirs I wrote and shared with others in honor of Serena over the years. No matter how many years pass, she will always hold a special place in our hearts: always loved, and never forgotten.

December 21, 2010

I saw this poem floating around on Facebook (author unknown) and posted in honor of Serena:

God saw you getting tired

And life outside the womb was not to be,

So He put his arms around you

And whispered "Come with Me."

With tearful eyes we watched

And knew you passed away

Although we love you dearly

We could not make you stay.

A precious heart stopped beating,

Pudgy little hands at rest,

God broke our hearts to prove to us

He only takes the best.

We will always miss our little girl. Serena Nadine.

2nd Birthday: July 28, 2011 (Facebook)

[Laura Story's *Blessings*] is particularly moving today, as I remember our precious daughter, Serena Nadine, on her 2nd anniversary. The daughter God used to teach me more than I ever realized I needed to know about Him and myself. Her life, though shorter than we expected or would have preferred and hoped, was not in the least bit in vain, and her mark is upon my life forever. I am so thankful God gave her to us and touched my life by her.

I look forward to the day I will see my little girl again and together we will worship the One who transforms our pain into blessings.

Serena's 3rd Birthday: July 28, 2012 (Journal Entry)

Three years... three years since my life was changed in a way I would never know. Three years since I held my first full-term child in my arms. Three years of ministering to other mothers who experience the loss of children. Three years of lessons learned. Three years of not being able to take the criticisms, strong opinions, and obnoxious ways of "certain people." Three years of learning more about God, His character, and how He operates and truly loves me. Three years of missing a part of our family. Three years of times of crying, blessing, pain, peace, loss, and love. Three years.

Back then, I would have never thought I would be at this place now. I wondered how I would ever smile again, or be happy about a pregnancy—what if I lost another one? I wondered if God really cared about me. I wondered if I'd feel His presence or His love. It was one day at a time, baby steps of progress. Lots of thinking, reading comforting passages or books and talking to God. I have come a long way, and I only write this to give hope to those who may later read this and be going through a loss too.

My cake topper for year three is: she no longer physically lives, but her memory lives on and continues to touch many lives. I see over and over how my experience with loss has helped me to have more compassion, sympathy, and thoughtfulness for those who experience the same or who are hurting.

Serena's 4th Birthday: July 28, 2013 (Facebook)

Remembering our precious little girl, Serena Nadine, who fulfilled all of the days the Lord had marked out for her and was given an express flight to heaven four years ago today. She is perfect, praising her Savior who gave His life so that she could live in heaven now in eternal peace and joy. Life would be much different if she were here with us, and she will always be loved and missed; never forgotten. Though she is dead to this world, she is very much alive in heaven. Her memory lives on through us, and the effect of her life and death is etched on our lives and our character forever. It wasn't a failed birth. It was a successful birth, completely in line with God's plan. It was a success because it completed God's plan for her life, or shall we say, it was just the beginning of a greater plan that He has.

Today, my heart goes out to my sisters in Christ, Marjie Canciglia and Sarah Isitt, who, in the past three months, were chosen by the Lord to do the hardest thing a mother must do—give her baby back to the Lord. Take heart, dear sisters. The Lord sees your pain, and He puts every one of those tears in a bottle. He will carry you through. He will heal your heart.

I pray that you will likewise know the peace and comfort that He has brought to our hearts in the loss of our Serena. The hole will always be there, but in time, a bridge is built over it. The wound will heal, but the scar will always remain.

He promises to work all things out for good for those who love Him, and I have seen Him do that for us. I believe with all my heart He will do it for you too.

Serena's 5th Birthday: July 28, 2014 (Facebook)

I am so blessed to be able to have this day to remember our precious first full-term baby girl, Serena Nadine, who was taken to be with Jesus during labor and delivery five years ago today. A precious little girl… and we are so blessed that she was a part of our lives, even for such a short time as she was taken so unexpectedly. God has used her, in death, in so many ways, teaching me many valuable lessons that I would never have learned had this never happened. He has fulfilled His promise to work out all things for good to those who love Him. He has given joy through tears, joy in the hope that we will see her again one day and together worship our Savior, the One who died so that she could live in eternal happiness, peace, and rest. Happy Heavenly Birthday to our precious little girl, Serena Nadine! Always missed, never forgotten and so thankful that she is spending this day praising Jesus!

I also want to acknowledge today those little ones who have also been given "express tickets" to heaven: Sarita Joy Feenstra, Alexandra Jo Barnhill, Ava Sophia Terlouw, Baby Beaudoin, Titus Gershom Liddle, Ella Marie Mowery, Levi Wrangler Lee, Elijah Mubezi, Isabella Joy Canciglia, Kendrah Grace Isitt, Arpan Saha, Allie Rae Mowery, Isaac Levi Parr, Gabriella Grigoryevna Dillingham, Judah Daniel Zwicker, Mahalani Lucy Prussic, and my two miscarried nieces/ nephews along with several others who experienced miscarriages (I hope I haven't missed anyone).

May the Lord continue to provide healing to their parents and family and may He also show them His amazing ability to bring joy out of mourning and His faithfulness to bless us with the peace that passes all understanding.

And a very happy birthday to Megan Burwell who was given life on this day, five years ago!

Serena's 6th Birthday: July 28, 2015 (Facebook)

July 28, 2009. It was a Tuesday, just like it is this year. Little did I know that it would be the most devastating day I would ever experience. Little did I know that our precious baby girl, Serena Nadine, would unexpectedly die during labor and delivery.

Six years have passed, and today, I look back over these six years, and I am grateful. Grateful for my precious baby girl whom God gave to me for a short time but whom He used to change me forever. Grateful that I can open my eyes this morning and smile with the hope and healing that He has granted. Grateful for the tears that wash the soul and nurture compassion for others in the same situation. Grateful for the precious children that He has blessed us with since those dark days. Grateful for the support of my dear husband through it all. Grateful for those who remember each year and who reach out to let me know. Grateful for all the lessons that the Lord has taught me through this most painful experience. Grateful for His patience, kindness, goodness, and love. Grateful for His hands that upheld me when my faith wasn't as strong as I would have liked or thought.

Most of all, I am grateful for Jesus, who willingly gave up His own life so that our Serena could now be in heaven with Him, free of pain, sin, and death, daily basking in His glorious presence! I am incredibly thankful for the hope in Jesus that her death was not the end—it is just the beginning! I am so looking forward in hope to seeing her again one day when I meet our loving and gentle Savior who does all things well, even when we don't understand. I am forever grateful He doesn't ask us to understand, but instead just to trust.

Our precious Serena; always loved and never forgotten.

Serena's 7th Birthday: July 28, 2016 (Facebook)

Seven years ago today, we laid the body of our first full-term baby, Serena Nadine, in the ground. We buried our hopes and dreams along with her precious little body, but at the same time, we are looking forward in hope to the resurrection and seeing her in heaven with Christ. Her birthday was last week, July 28th, and I penned some thoughts that I hope will be a blessing to you as you grieve the loss of your own child:

"Seven years. Often the number seven is associated with completeness. But, in the deepest recesses of my heart, completeness seems to be the furthest description for our family. As I think back to the moment the doctor looked at me and said, 'The baby is dead; the heart chambers are not moving,' to that dark hospital room where I whispered goodbye to my first baby girl who lay silent on the bed; as I watched my father and husband carry her little white casket across the cemetery grass and then lower it into the ground, and as I watched my nine-year-old brother walk over and take the shovel to scoop up some dirt and pour it onto her casket, the feeling of completeness was nowhere on the horizon.

With each child that the Lord blesses us with, and as we take family photos, there is always 'the spot' where she would be standing or sitting. There is always the question from strangers of, 'So what number is this one?' when I am expecting another baby, and my heart refuses to leave her out of the count. At times, there are days when I am certain I am missing a child somewhere in the house, but when I take a headcount, all of them are there—the living ones, that is. When I look at the photos of the grandchildren, the very first grand-daughter and the very first grandchild for my parents is always missing. There are still tears. There is still the longing to hold her one more time, to kiss those chubby cheeks and feel her small fingers around my own finger. There is the wondering of what she would be like, what kinds of things she would be doing, and how her life here would change the whole dynamic of our family.

And yet, in the midst of all the incompleteness I feel, there *is* completeness. She is perfectly complete. She has perfect happiness, perfect joy, perfect love, and perfect peace. She beholds our perfect Savior day after day. She doesn't know the pain of disobedience, the pain of rejection, or the hardships of life. She has no disappointments, no regrets, no suffering. She is free—all because of our Savior whose sacrifice was complete, whose blood was shed to satisfy the debt that we all owe to God for our sins. Without His complete sacrifice, I would have no hope now. Her death would be the end of the story. But because of Him, her death was just the beginning—a beginning of an eternity of peace, joy, rest and security. Because of Him, I have hope that one day, I will see her again. And it is my prayer that the Lord will draw all of our children to Himself. I look forward to finally knowing, humanly speaking, what it is like to have a complete family.

But for now, and especially today on her 7th birthday, dear Jesus, would You wrap Serena in Your loving arms and whisper in her ear that her Mama loves her so much and thinks of her all the time? Would You let her know how much I would love for her to be here with our family and yet how blessed I am that she is there with You? Would You let her know that she is never forgotten and how much she means to our family? Would You let her know that her brothers and sisters talk about her and look forward to meeting her one day? Would You let her know that one day, I will be there with her to worship You for all eternity?

And for those who are reading this and have lost their own little ones, may your heart be comforted by the One who can only give us complete joy and peace in this life. May you know the peace that passes all understanding and may He show you the perfect plan that He has for your life, even as you feel the incompleteness of your family. One day, the things of this life will be forgotten for the glories that we will experience in heaven. There will be no more tears, no more pain, no more sorrow... and no more 'goodbyes.'"

Serena's 8th Birthday: "She Lives On" (The ELLA Foundation Facebook page; email to family and friends)

Eight years ago. July 28, 2009. The day that changed my life forever. The day I would hold my first full-term daughter but have to give her back in that same day to Christ. It was the darkest day of my life, but little did I know that it would be that darkest day that would produce the brightest transformation.

As I think back over this past year, it seems like it has been one of the easiest years—not because I feel like I have "gotten over" her death; not because I have five living children and another little one on the way, and not because enough time has passed that the sting isn't there anymore. I feel like this year has been one of the easiest years because I have had an increasing number of opportunities to share the hope and transformation we have in Christ because our precious Serena is in heaven.

When I think back to those awful days, weeks and months following her death, I could have never envisioned the impact that her story would have for years to come. I think of the Mormons who came to our door in the past year and in the course of the conversation, I was able to share with them the hope that we have and how God keeps His people through the most difficult circumstances in life because of the personal experience I had with her loss. I think of my neighbor with whom I can share the hope that we have as I talk about our little girl and reminisce on the precious memories that I have of her. I think of the store clerks, customer service representatives, complete strangers, family members, brothers and sisters in God's family who are undergoing difficult circumstances... all of whom are touched by the impact that our little girl has made in our lives, by God's grace.

This year I realized that it isn't only bereaved mothers and fathers, grandparents and family members that are touched by our little girl's life and death; she touches the lives of others who are going through hardships because of what God worked in her parents' lives by her brief time on earth. Every time I walk away from a conversation with someone where they were impacted because of what we went through, I marvel and sincerely thank the

Lord for how He worked something so wonderful—something that I could have never imagined.

Something special for this year was that I realized just how sweet it is to celebrate her birthday—a special day where I can formally acknowledge her when every other day of the year, her absence is felt. The hard times come at different points throughout the year, but this day, July 28th, is "Serena's birthday." Our children look forward to it. This year, they counted down the days leading up to it. Our family traditions include visiting the cemetery together as a family, taking photos in front of her gravestone, celebrating her perfect life with Christ with Jamba Juice smoothies and birthday cake and watching the slideshow of the few photos we have of her. There are a lot of questions, and it is sweet to hear the children talk about how they wish Serena were here. I am real with them and confess that I wish she was here too, but that I am so happy that we know where she is, safe with Jesus, perfect and free from sin and all the consequences of it. We talk about the joy that she has, how infinitely better heaven is than anything we could ever possibly enjoy here, and we turn their eyes to focus on Christ and the goodness that He has bestowed on us.

Eight years ago, there was nothing of this nature. Just horrible pain, deep anguish, despair and hopelessness that threatened to drown me. This year, our eldest son took a photo of only my husband and me in front of Serena's grave. As I looked at it, my mind drifted back to the burial service and the photos that were taken of us during that time. Indescribable pain was deeply written on our faces. Unspeakable grief. That day, I would have never dreamed of being able to smile again or have my arms so full of blessings. All I felt was the dark cloud surrounding me. But now, I am looking at my husband and myself this year, in front of her grave, and it is something that I can't find words to adequately describe! God has done wondrous things in our lives. I am so very grateful. Yes, I still shed my tears, and likely always will, but He truly does give a peace that passes all understanding.

Another special thing this year is that the Lord brought two children into my life in the past four months who are just about the same age as Serena would be. One child is a young boy who was born July 22nd, and the other is a girl who is born exactly one month after Serena, on August 28th. As I look at these children, especially the young girl, a smile creeps across my face as I think of what our Serena would be like right now. Life would be so different. Caleb wouldn't be the eldest child. There would be a lot of different dynamics in our family with her being a living part of it. But I also would not be the same person that I am today because of her loss and the wonders that God worked in my life because of her death.

I just want to conclude this post by saying that for those of you who are in the trenches right now; where the loss is recent or still very painful; where the ache feels like it will never go away; where the cloud feels like it will never pass and the sun won't ever shine again; where the anniversary of your child's death is dark and dreary and you dread every day of the month that leads up to it, be encouraged. The day will come where you will smile again; where you can look forward to your child's birthday as you can formally celebrate the life that they enjoy with Christ; where you can see the sunshine and allow the rays of hope to beam onto those around you who are struggling with the challenges of life; where you can experience the peace that passes all understanding—all of this only because of Christ, His sacrifice, and the incomprehensible love that He has for His people. He is in the business of taking the darkest situations of life and transforming them into the most radiant beams of joy and hope that one cannot imagine.

Serena's 9th Birthday: July 28, 2018 (Journal Entry)

Nine years have passed. Really? Some days it feels like it is just a memory and that it never really happened to me. And, yet deep down inside, she is woven into every part of my being. This year, Caleb and Nadine wanted to bake her birthday cake and decorate it. I was delighted to see how excited they were to celebrate their big sister that they never met.

This month, I was blessed to be able to take in nine bereavement gowns to Barton's Funeral Home in an effort to bring a bit of sweetness to parents when they are faced with the death of their little one. I was hoping that Overlake Hospital would be willing to accept gowns as well, but they have to get permission from the volunteer department, and that hasn't happened at the moment. Hopefully, it will be soon.

This year, I was focusing on bringing comfort and healing to a couple that lost their baby girl last year on July 24th. I baked a cake and drove up to Marysville with the kiddos to let this couple know that their little girl was remembered and acknowledged. Perhaps that is why this year seemed a bit different for me as well. I felt so much lighter, and a sense of peace just washed over me on this day. Focusing on serving others helps to alleviate the pain, and when I see how Serena's life and death impacts others, I can't help but smile and thank the Lord for the beauty He has brought out of ashes.

Oh Lord, thank You, thank You for your faithfulness to Your promises. Thank You for every one of the little ones You have given to me here and thank You for Your sacrifice so that Serena can be in heaven with You along with Baby Gad, Baby Ezekiel, and Baby Dara, knowing the peace and joy that only comes in Your presence. May You continue to use Serena for Your glory and the benefit of others!

Please note: there have been some slight modifications made to these original postings for readability.

Appendix

Personal Questions and Answers

Over the years, I have had different questions/topics asked of me by grieving mothers. I thought it might be helpful to share a few in case you might be asking the same ones, seeking an answer from someone who has undergone the same trial you are walking through now.

Please keep in mind that everyone and every situation is different. What is true for me might not be true for you, so please know that I am simply sharing my own experience in hopes of offering encouragement and standing with you.

1. **How long was it before the sting went away?**

   I don't remember the exact moment it went away, but I do remember an entire year passing before I felt that deep pain assuage. I think part of it had to do with passing the one year mark, knowing that I could actually live through that utterly life-changing, devastating day. In any case, give yourself time. Right now, a year might feel like a long time, but I promise the sting *will* go away.

2. Does God love me less because He took my baby but gave my friend theirs?

Satan would love to make us believe that the reason God took our baby from us is that He doesn't love us as much as someone else. Nothing could be farther from the truth. Our Father reminds us that whom the Lord loves, He chastens. If He leaves you without discipline, it is as if you are an illegitimate child. *"And ye have forgotten the exhortation which speaketh unto you as unto children, My son, despise not thou the chastening of the Lord, nor faint when thou art rebuked of Him: For whom the Lord loveth He chasteneth, and scourgeth every son whom He receiveth. If ye endure chastening, God dealeth with you as with sons; for what son is he whom the father chasteneth not? But if ye be without chastisement, whereof all are partakers, then are ye bastards, and not sons. Furthermore, we have had fathers of our flesh which corrected us, and we gave them reverence: shall we not much rather be in subjection unto the Father of spirits, and live? For they verily for a few days chastened us after their own pleasure; but He for our profit, that we might be partakers of His holiness. Now no chastening for the present seemeth to be joyous, but grievous: nevertheless afterward it yieldeth the peaceable fruit of righteousness unto them which are exercised thereby."* (Hebrews 11:5-11)

Please know that I am not saying that the reason your child died was that God was disciplining you. Job's life is a clear reminder that suffering happens even when you haven't done anything specifically wrong. However, if God assures us of His love in a situation of discipline, how much more can you be assured of His love for you if this is *not* a situation of discipline!

This is something that is incredibly hard to wrap your mind around, but maybe it is helpful to think of it in the opposite way—what if God loves you *more* because He wants to give you a taste of the glories of heaven, deeper fellowship with Him, and is weaning you from the attachment to this world? What if He is developing a deeper and stronger faith in Him that will withstand all opposition? What if He is making you trust and rely on Him and giving you the freedom that comes from learning to let go rather than desperately holding on to the things of this life?

Maybe it would be helpful to think of the fact that your baby is assured its entrance into heaven. We don't know if each of our living children will follow the Lord and be found worshipping Him eternally in heaven. But for those that He has taken to be with Him, we can have the assurance that they are there for eternity and you will see them again.

Try to ponder the glories that your baby is experiencing now rather than the things they would have had to endure in this sinful world. I know that a huge part of us still wants our baby here even with all of the things that happen in a fallen world, but if you can ask God to help you focus on the wonderful glories that your baby is experiencing rather than focusing on the things that you are missing out on by their absence, it can help to alleviate the pain and transform this devastation into beauty.

This quote by Matthew Henry was included by our pastor in the bulletin for Serena's burial. "Though your children are early removed from this world, surely there is no harm done, for the time they have lost on earth they have gained in heaven." (The Complete Works of Matthew Henry, Volume 1, p.561,562)

3. **How do I give the pain to Jesus?**

    From my experience, I feel that giving your pain to Jesus is not a step-by-step process, nor does it have a simple formula. I think it consists of praying to Him and laying your heart out before Him every day, and being completely transparent. I think it consists of being humble before Him and asking Him to help you do what you know He wants you to do. It is stepping out and choosing to do what you know the Lord desires of you, even when you don't feel like it.

4. **I am scared... What else will God take away from me?**

    I definitely struggled with this after miscarrying our first, losing Serena during labor and then miscarrying our third. I wondered if God would ever give me a living child. I felt like my womb was a grave. I knew that He could keep every child alive... but He wasn't.

    I dealt with a lot of fears. Fear of His power. Fear of His sovereignty. I had to come to the place where I surrendered to His will for my life, no matter what it entailed. I had to be willing to give up my plans, my desires, my dreams and my vision for the life I wanted to have with a large family, serving the Lord. It was as if He was teaching me that He could glorify Himself in whatever way He chose—whether that be through giving me a living child, or taking that child away. It was only when I was willing to say, "Not my will but Thine be done" that the peace would come. And it takes time. Be patient with yourself, but let the prayer of your heart be, "Lord, help me to truly be able to say, 'Not my will, but Thine be done.'"

5. **God says He gives good gifts to His children. Then why did He take away my baby—isn't that a good gift? Why did He withhold that from me?**

    This goes along with some of the things I have already written. Yes, having a new baby is truly a beautiful gift from the Lord. But how many women of God struggled with barrenness? Sarah, Rebekah, Hannah, and Elizabeth. Just as we don't choose to give our children all the same gift but tailor our gifts to what they need or enjoy or would benefit most by, so it is with the Lord. He tailors the gifts that He gives to each of His children so that they can be blessed in the richest of ways. We, of course, don't see it that way, just as a child may whine and complain that he didn't get a set of bouncy balls like his brother did or a doll set like her sister received. It seems to me that we have to learn to open our eyes to the beauty of the gift that God has given to us, even when it feels like a knife in our heart. We need to focus on the beautiful rose rather than the sharp thorn that poked into our hand when the rose was handed to us. Sometimes God seeks to give us the greater gift, so He withholds the great so that He can give us the greatest.

6. **Did you have sleepless nights for weeks at a time?**

    In the first couple of weeks after we lost Serena, I would awake from nightmares where I kept hearing, "Push! Push!" I'd get ripped out of my sleep only to relive the memories again and cry (and cry some more) myself back to sleep. I was constantly exhausted from sorrow. Even still, I don't feel like I experienced nights where I would be up for three-four hours at a time, for weeks on end. A friend of mine was asking me about that, and while I pondered the question, I realized that she has three young girls to care for during the day. Perhaps she endured sleepless nights because she is too distracted with tending to their needs that she doesn't have time during the day to grieve, so the grieving comes at night when it is quiet and she is alone with her thoughts. Because we had no other children when we lost Serena, I spent the daytime grieving so by the time the night came, I was exhausted with sorrow and didn't have too difficult a time falling asleep.

If you find that this is happening to you, while I don't feel well qualified to address a remedy for this, when I suffered from sleeplessness as a teenager due to some relationship challenges that were occurring around me, I would get up and read the Psalms—specifically 34, 37, and 73. Psalm 34 and 37 are full of God's promises to His people, and Psalm 73 deals with being envious at the wicked who seem to prosper while the righteous are afflicted. The only way that the psalmist found relief was "going into the sanctuary of God," and then he understood.

I find that it is the same for us as well. We can look around and think that things are incredibly unfair, wondering why this happened to us and questioning why others have their babies, but when we enter the presence of the Lord, He gives us understanding. Whether it is an understanding of our situation, or just an understanding that He has it all under control, the understanding comes. And therein, you can find peace.

7. **I feel like Satan is warring against me and really attacking my mind; did you experience this?**

Oh yes! I feel like Satan takes advantage of our weakened state with grief to strike with every weapon he has. He sends the Demon of Doubt, the Fiend of Unforgiveness, the Rogue of Resentment, the Witch of Wrath, the Demon of Distrust, the Demon of Discontentment, the Spirit of Self-Pity, the Spirit of Strife and every one of his host to plague us, beat us down and make us turn away from God.

He sends his fiery darts that we have to quench with the shield of faith. I found that fighting Satan with Scripture was helpful, but there were also days when I was just so weary of the fight. I felt like just throwing myself at Jesus' feet in exhaustion and giving up. But what kept me going was this thought: "I can't let Satan win. What if he has challenged God about me just like he did about Job? I can't let him laugh in the face of God, not after all Jesus did to save me." So, once again, I would get back up, pleading with God for help to fight the battle. Gradually, the fight decreased, and the attack didn't come as often. As long as I bathed my mind in the truths of God's Word and focused on those truths rather than the lies Satan was telling me, the battle became less and less vehement.

8. **Were there special things that you began to help you process the grief?**

When we first lost Serena, I found that I gravitated toward expressing my grief through art. I hadn't had any formal art lessons, just some weekly lessons for a short time before I was married with an adopted "Oma" at church. Even though the lessons weren't formal, all that she taught me was very helpful as I spent many days and weeks in the quiet of our basement suite, painting scenes that depicted the state of my heart and reminding myself of the truths that I knew but didn't feel.

As the Lord brought bereaved mothers into my life, I began painting name plaques in memory of the babies that passed into glory. I also started making bibs for teddy bears and personalizing them with the baby's name and date on it. In August 2017, I began transforming donated wedding gowns into bereavement gowns. I am not a seamstress by any stretch, but I knew how blessed I would have been to receive a beautiful gown for Serena in the hospital and wanted other grieving parents to have a small glimpse of sweetness in the pain they were facing.

Using a free online pattern, and my meager sewing skills, I stepped out in faith, and a new facet of ministry was born.

Within a year's time, 45 gowns had been designed and sewn, many of which were donated to hospitals in Michigan and funeral homes here in Washington. Here are a few of the gowns that have been made and donated to hospitals and funeral homes.

If you would like a gown as a keepsake, please message me at

abridgeofhope1@gmail.com.

I would love to send you one.

9. **How long was it before you stopped the rollercoaster of being composed one moment and then finding yourself uncontrollably weeping the next?**

My situation was a bit unique because I had moved to Washington state from Canada when my husband and

I married in June of 2008. We were new members of a very small church, and my husband was so busy with establishing his new business that we didn't have much of social life. I am also of a shyer disposition and didn't reach out a lot and make new friends. Not to mention my family was all out of the country. That said, I feel like I spent a lot of time at home, and alone. I didn't have a whole lot of opportunities for breaking down in public settings. I did experience situations where the strangest things would turn on the grief, but I encourage you that those times of sudden "breaking down" will become farther and farther apart as time goes by. Once again, be patient with yourself.

10. **God says joy comes in the morning, but it seems like I am not finding it.**

Yes, the Lord says, "Weeping may endure for a night, but joy cometh in the morning." However, sometimes that night is prolonged. It doesn't always mean the next morn-

ing. If that were the case in the death of a child, especially an unexpected death, I don't think the depth of love could (or would) be perceived. It seems that the vast amount of time that it takes to grieve the loss of a precious child indicates just how deep and rich the love was to begin with.

Joy coming in the morning can sometimes be found in the things that we least expect. Finding joy in God's mercy and His care and His preservation during this time can be one aspect of joy. Oftentimes, we limit our vision to the things that we expect to receive from what God promises us, but I encourage you to open your eyes to see the tiniest things that will show you that God is indeed faithful to every one of His promises. These tiny mercies could be in the form of a good night of sleep, a helpful conversation, a gesture of kindness from a friend, or neighbor, the ability to actually smile once again, and more.

"There failed not ought of any good thing which the LORD had spoken unto the house of Israel; all came to pass." (Joshua 21:45)

11. **Is there a special memory that stands out to you after the time of devastation where you really saw the hand of the Lord?**

Definitely! One special story that I love to share is the birth of our 1st living child, Caleb Jeremiah. He was due on September 15, 2010, exactly two years from the date that I miscarried our first baby, Baby Gad, at eleven-and-a-half weeks. When I found out my due date with Caleb was September 15th, I asked the Lord to bring the baby on its due date, to turn that day of mourning into a day of joy, if that were His will. I well knew that babies rarely come on their due dates, but I also knew the Lord could do so if He chose.

September 14th came, and I had just finished giving my husband a haircut. I prepared for a night of sleep and was wondering if the baby would arrive the next day. I felt a sudden tightening of my pelvic area, and it wasn't long before the first contractions began. Could it be true?! This baby could definitely be born on the 15th.

And so it was! At 1:17 PM, Caleb Jeremiah made his entrance into the world. God took the day that had been a day of devastation and turned it into a day of rejoicing. And, for the record, all five of our children since then have been born "late." Without a doubt, I feel it was a clear answer to my prayer from the Lord.

12. **What were some of the hardest practical things you faced after you lost Serena?**

I think the hardest thing was not being able to talk to her anymore. After nine months of talking to her daily, having her with me every waking moment, to suddenly not have her there anymore was horrible. I felt like I never really had a chance to process the fact that she was not going to be with me anymore. I never told her "goodbye," really. To help me get through this tough part, I would talk to Jesus and ask Him to tell her everything that I wanted to say to her. That way, I felt the reality that the relationship had changed—she was no longer alive in this world—and my focus was on Christ.

Another difficult thing was seeing all of the other babies born during that time and not having my baby in my arms. To help me get through this, I felt that I needed to put myself in situations where I would face the pain head-on and heal through it. My husband knew a couple from the church he previously attended that welcomed their baby girl, Megan, on the exact day that Serena died. A mutual friend offered for me to go over and visit the family and hold the baby... *if* I wanted to do something like that. While some people may have thought I was out of my mind, I knew it was something that I needed to do to help me heal. On Thursday, October 15, 2009, I drove down to Renton to meet this little girl who shared the exact same birthday as Serena.

When I arrived, Megan was napping, but she awoke after a while and her mother, Corrie, was so willing to let me hold her. I will never forget that first moment that Megan was in my arms. Corrie gave me a little space with her, and I remember talking to Megan quietly but can't remember anything I said. We shared birth stories as Corrie nursed Megan, and we shed tears. I went home and cried some more, but I really feel like facing the pain and reaching out to acknowledge and celebrate the life of a little girl born on the exact same day as my little girl was a piece in the puzzle of healing that God was bringing in my life. Every year, I send either a note to Megan's parents (when she was younger) or a card in the mail now that she is older to let her know we are thinking of her and thankful for the life the Lord granted to her.

I did the same with my nephew, who was born the month before Serena. Though there were times that it was painful and I would come home and cry after seeing him, it was an important part of the healing. I feel that distancing myself would have only caused the pain to take root, and resentment to spring up, whereas facing it helped my wound to be "disinfected" and heal. I don't remember how long it was before the pain went away when seeing him (they also lived two hours north of us, so we didn't see them all that often), but I think that after a couple of years, the sting had disappeared. I think he was two or three-years-old when he was sitting beside me on the porch swing, and I could genuinely smile as I looked into his cute face. I distinctly remember when we were up for his sixth birthday celebration, and I hugged him goodbye. I squeezed him close to me with a sense of sweet joy, being grateful that he gives me a glimpse of just how big she would be now.

I also realized that signing cards was difficult because I had always added "and the baby on the way" to the greeting cards I sent to family members. (If you recall, my family lived in Canada, and we used the postal system to send birthday cards to each other.) Now I had no name to put after Elliott's and my name. Finally, I decided after we had at least Caleb, to sign our greetings cards with a ... before Caleb's name. It has stuck!

13. **What was it like for you after you had a living child?**

When Caleb was born alive and crying, I cried too—tears of joy and tears of knowing just what I had missed out on with Serena. Throughout that first year with him, I continued to grieve, enjoying all of the special things he did and watching him learn and develop, but I definitely wiped away tears thinking of what I never experienced with Serena and what he would never experience with her as well. I think that all of the "new mother" challenges that many experience were not a problem for me because I was just so thankful that I had a baby to hold in my arms, to love on and to keep on this side of heaven.

14. **What worked to keep your marriage together in rough times?**

I alluded to the fact that I don't really feel all that adequate to answer this question, but here is the answer that one of my friends gave when I sought her advice in response to another grieving mother's question of me:

"As for the woman who lost her two-year-old son, my heart

just aches! The best advice for her in regards to her marriage is to communicate. I can't stress that enough. They are both grieving differently, and they need to make sure they don't criticize each other on how they grieve or get upset with each other. If something is bothering her or him or they are having a "bad" day, they need to tell each other so they can support each other and know they can count on each other, NO MATTER WHAT! Don't keep it in.

I am not sure if they have other children or not, but I found the demands of caring for the boys and the responsibilities of everyday life—and A with his job—don't stop. As much as you want the world to stop just for a moment because your life has fallen apart, to take a break with just the two of them, it just doesn't. A and I went away for a week, to 'get away' from it all and *really* communicate. I could tell him what was really on my heart and how certain things he said were so hurtful even though they were so unintentional. He was going to try and be more understanding, supportive and non-judgmental, as was I. It was a way to reconnect, to talk, listen, and pray for each other."

15. **Were there any special mementos that you got in memory of Serena?**

After we lost Serena in July, around October, Elliott and I began shopping around for a ring that would have a ruby (her birthstone) in it. We found one that was suitable, and I have worn it every day since then.

This past year, for our 10th anniversary, Elliott had a mother's necklace designed for me, and he included Serena's birthstone on there as well. It is such a sweet reminder that she holds a special place in my heart, just as all of our children do.

I also made "prayer bracelets" this year to help me pray daily for our children. I made one with Serena's name on it as well, and when I come to her name, I use it as an opportunity to pray for grieving parents and to thank the Lord for how He used her in my life.

16. **How do you handle family photos?**

This was a tough one for me because I always felt like someone was missing in our photos. I could always see "the spot" where she would have been sitting or standing. So, I decided to use the teddy bear that was given to us by Barton Funeral Homes in her place. Now, in our professional family portraits, we include Serena's bear. I am fairly "hardcore" about the bear being in the photos. This past year, I even asked to re-shoot the pose when her bear was forgotten on the stroller, and no one had it in their hands! And be assured, re-shooting the pose with six kids ages seven and under is no easy task, but the photographer was amazing. I just feel like having the bear in the photo helps to fill the "hole."

17. **You mentioned that you went to a Women's Conference the October after you lost Serena, which was just what you needed. Are there any "nuggets" you can share from that conference?**

Yes! *Strength for Life's Struggles* was held on October 16th and 17th, 2009, and Mary Esvelt was the main speaker. While I had tears running down my face for most of the sessions, it was just what I needed. It touched my heart so intimately. Mary's son, Seth, was severely injured in an automobile accident in 2003, leaving him 100% dependent on them. He was classified as minimally conscious/vegetative. Mary shared the painful lessons that she learned through the tragedy that struck their family and blessed my heart.

Here are a few points from the notes I took during that conference:

* Know Him and love Him for who He is, not for what He gives or what He does.

* If God took our son home, we would be thankful for the 23 years we had with him. If God allowed him to live, God would give grace to us.

* Don't live by your feelings; live by faith.

* Sometimes the invisible hand of God is working in the background, working out His plan. We never know what He is doing.

  ♦ I will add here that just this week, I heard someone say, "Just because God is silent doesn't mean that He is not working. He is working something behind the scenes that we cannot see. We need to trust Him."

* If God doesn't fulfill what we want, are we still able to worship Him? Trust Him?

* Some days I feel like I just can't go on. "Lord, give me the grace and love to serve others for You. You have to give me the grace to live with sorrow, sadness, grief and loss and still radiate Your joy."

* Be faithful in the small things: reading the Word, prayer, sharing, serving.

* Perseverance is the ability to remain under the circumstances you are in without giving up.

* Are we going to become bitter or better?

* Are we going to be burned or are we going to be refined?

* Because we believe in God's sovereignty, does that mean we won't struggle? God's people do struggle.

* Sometimes you think the grieving is over, but something else causes an added dimension to your grief. It hits at the most unexpected times.

* Be willing to have deaths in your life so that others may have life and benefit.

* Do you feel that God has given you a cruel blow?

  1. Read Scripture and memorize it.

  2. Read godly biographies—those where you see a person going through pain and suffering and making it through.

  3. Spend time with godly people.

  4. Pick out a life verse.

* Often we are billboards and we don't know it.

* "Light affliction"—*now* it doesn't seem to be light, but then (in heaven) it will be.

* In eternity, it will be worth it all.

* Conclusion of the Matter:

1. Fear God, keep His commandments.

2. Be careful about how you live. You don't know what will happen tomorrow.

3. Teach me to number my days that I may apply my heart to wisdom.

* Live with integrity and joy, bringing glory to God.

18. **Are there any particular portions of Scripture that you found especially helpful when grieving?**

Yes, I found the Psalms to be very helpful for me as I grieved. In particular, I found Psalm 13, 55, 56, 72 and 77 very applicable to how I was feeling. Also, reading the Gospels, especially John, where it shows the love and compassion that Jesus has for His people, even when they suffer, ministered to my heart. Accounts of Bible characters that underwent a lot of suffering (Israel in Egypt, Job, David, Joseph, Naomi, and Ruth) were also of profound encouragement to me. I took time to sit and really ponder what I was reading, putting myself in their situation, and noting how they responded to their situation.

19. **Are there certain songs that really ministered to you after you lost Serena?**

It is interesting that even though I am a professional musician, I didn't listen to a lot of music or songs when we lost Serena. I wasn't acquainted with a lot of the contemporary Christian songs out there at the time, but I have come across several over the past years when I am ministering to others in their pain and the lyrics speak to many of the things I felt and experienced. I know everyone's music preferences and standards are different, so please take these songs as suggestions based on their lyrics. :)

Hymns

- *Day by Day*
- *God Will Take Care of You*
- *Does Jesus Care?*
- *If Thou but Suffer God to Guide Thee*

Psalter Selections

- *Quieting Thoughts* (Psalter 7- Psalm 4)
- *The Secret of Tranquility* (Psalter 100 - Psalm 37)
- *Desire for Rest* (Psalter 150 - Psalm 55)
- *The Good Shepherd* (Psalter 55 - Psalm 23)

Classical

- Pavane for A Dead Princess (Gabriel Faure)

Contemporary Christian

- *Glory Baby* (Watermark)
- *He Will Carry You* (Gaither Vocal Band)
- *In the Valley* (Bob Kauflin)
- *I Will Praise You in the Storm* (Casting Crowns)
- *Even If* (MercyMe)
- *Thy Will be Done* (Hillary Scott)

- *Blessings* (Laura Story)
- *Need You Now* (Plumb)
- *I Will Carry You* (Selah)
- *Just Be Held* (Casting Crowns)
- *Safely Home* (Casting Crowns)
- *In the Hands of the Potter* (Casting Crowns)

Western

- *I Drive Your Truck* (Lee Brice)

  Note: this one speaks to the raw feelings of grief; when I first heard this song recently, it reminded me of the "big, ugly cry" that we feel rising from the deepest cell of our body often in grief. You know, the kind where you want to double over, hoping that somehow if you could scream it all out, the pain won't sear through your being anymore.

20. **Were there certain books that you found helpful?**

    Yes, I did. Here are some of the titles that I recall:

    * *Faithful God* by Sinclair Ferguson

    * *When Heaven is Silent* by Ron Dunn

    * *I'll Hold You in Heaven - Remembrance Book* by Debbie Heydrick

    * *Trusting God Even When Life Hurts* by Jerry Bridges

    * *My Utmost for His Highest* by Oswald Chambers (devotional)

    * *Trusting God in a Twisted World* by Elisabeth Eliot

    * *Faith's Checkbook* by Charles Spurgeon

21. **Would you recommend biographies that helped you as you dealt with your pain?**

I think that *The Hiding Place* by Corrie Ten Boom always helps to put suffering into perspective. Sometimes it helps to read about others' pain to realize that we aren't the only ones in the world who are going through terrible pain and also to see how they came through it victorious and lived a fruitful life thereafter. I recently watched The Torchlighter's DVD on Corrie's life with our children, and the attitude that Betsy consistently displays about being thankful for everything, not hating their persecutors, etc. really spoke to my heart as to how we ought to respond to the pain the Lord brings in to our lives. Also, the life of Elisabeth Elliot would be helpful in learning to navigate suffering and trials, using them to glorify the Lord rather than causing us to be stale and unfruitful.

Verses That Speak to Our Heart

Sometimes when we are going through such depth of grief, we don't know what to pray. We don't feel like reading the Word of God. We don't feel like doing anything but crawling under blankets, closing our eyes and falling into a sleep that we only hope to awaken from if our life is what it was like before tragedy struck.

But I want to encourage you, even if you don't feel like praying, pray. Even if you don't feel like reading God's Word, read it. In its pages, you will find that the saints of old also underwent deep suffering and pain, and their experience will minister comfort to you that is invaluable. The promises of God, though at times don't feel like they are meant for you, will bathe your mind with truth and help you to overcome the fiery darts from Satan.

Here are a few of the verses that helped and strengthened me as I walked through this valley.

Feelings of Despair

"My God, my God, why hast Thou forsaken me? why art Thou so far from helping me, and from the words of my roaring? O my God, I cry in the day time, but Thou hearest not; and in the night season, and am not silent. But Thou art holy, O Thou that inhabitest the praises of Israel.

Our fathers trusted in Thee: they trusted, and Thou didst deliver them. They cried unto Thee, and were delivered: they trusted in Thee, and were not confounded. " (Psalm 22:1-5)

"How long wilt Thou forget me, O Lord? For ever? how long wilt Thou hide Thy face from me? How long shall I take counsel in my soul, having sorrow in my heart daily? how long shall mine enemy be exalted over me? Consider and hear me, O Lord my God: lighten mine eyes, lest I sleep the sleep of death; Lest mine enemy say, I have prevailed against him; and those that trouble me rejoice when I am moved. But I have trusted in Thy mercy; my heart shall rejoice in Thy salvation. I will sing unto the Lord, because He hath dealt bountifully with me. " (Psalm 13)

"O Lord God of my salvation, I have cried day and night before Thee: Let my prayer come before Thee: incline Thine ear unto my cry; For my soul is full of troubles: and my life draweth nigh unto the grave. I am counted with them that go down into the pit: I am as a man that hath no strength: Free among the dead, like the slain that lie in the grave, whom Thou rememberest no more: and they are cut off from Thy hand. Thou hast laid me in the lowest pit, in darkness, in the deeps. Thy wrath lieth hard upon me, and Thou hast afflicted me with all Thy waves. Selah. Thou hast put away mine acquaintance far from me; Thou hast made me an abomination unto them: I am shut up, and I cannot come forth. Mine eye mourneth by reason of affliction: Lord, I have called daily upon Thee, I have stretched out my hands unto Thee. Wilt Thou shew wonders to the dead? shall the dead arise and praise Thee? Selah. Shall Thy lovingkindness be declared in the grave? or Thy faithfulness in destruction? Shall Thy wonders be known in the dark? and Thy righteousness in the land of forgetfulness? But unto Thee have I cried, O Lord; and in the morning shall my prayer prevent Thee. Lord, why castest Thou off my soul? why hidest Thou Thy face from me? I am

afflicted and ready to die from my youth up: while I suffer Thy terrors I am distracted. Thy fierce wrath goeth over me; Thy terrors have cut me off. They came round about me daily like water; they compassed me about together. Lover and friend hast Thou put far from me, and mine acquaintance into darkness." (Psalm 88)

Fear

"What time I am afraid, I will trust in Thee." (Psalm 56:3)

"But now thus saith the Lord that created thee, O Jacob, and He that formed thee, O Israel, Fear not: for I have redeemed thee, I have called thee by thy name; thou art Mine. When thou passest through the waters, I will be with thee; and through the rivers, they shall not overflow thee: when thou walkest through the fire, thou shalt not be burned; neither shall the flame kindle upon thee." (Isaiah 43:1-2)

"Say to them that are of a fearful heart, Be strong, fear not: behold, your God will come with vengeance, even God with a recompence; He will come and save you." (Isaiah 35:4)

Trust

"For the Lord God will help me; therefore shall I not be confounded: therefore have I set my face like a flint, and I know that I shall not be ashamed. He is near that justifieth me; who will contend with me? let us stand together: who is mine adversary? let him come near to me. Behold, the Lord God will help me; who is he that shall condemn me? lo, they all shall wax old as a garment; the moth shall eat them up. Who is among you that feareth the Lord, that obeyeth the voice of his servant, that walketh in darkness, and hath no light? let him trust in the name of the Lord, and stay upon his God." (Isaiah 50:7-10)

"Trust in the Lord, with all thine heart; and lean not unto thine own understanding. In all thy ways, acknowledge Him, and He shall direct your paths." (Proverbs 3:5,6)

"Trust in the Lord, and do good; so shalt thou dwell in the land, and verily thou shalt be fed." (Psalm 37:3)

Joy in Suffering

"Although the fig tree shall not blossom, neither shall fruit be in the vines; the labour of the olive shall fail, and the fields shall yield no meat; the flock shall be cut off from the fold, and there shall be no herd in the stalls: Yet I will rejoice in the Lord, I will joy in the God of my salvation. The Lord God is my strength, and He will make my feet like hinds' feet, and He will make me to walk upon mine high places. To the chief singer on my stringed instruments." (Habakkuk 3:17-19)

"Wherein ye greatly rejoice, though now for a season, if need be, ye are in heaviness through manifold temptations: That the trial of your faith, being much more precious than of gold that perisheth, though it be tried with fire, might be found unto praise and honour and glory at the appearing of Jesus Christ:" (I Peter 1:6-7)

"Beloved, think it not strange concerning the fiery trial which is to try you, as though some strange thing happened unto you: But rejoice, inasmuch as ye are partakers of Christ's sufferings; that, when His glory shall be revealed, ye may be glad also with exceeding joy." (I Peter 4:12-13)

God Hears Our Cries

"For the people shall dwell in Zion at Jerusalem: thou shalt weep no more: He will be very gracious unto thee at the voice of thy cry; when He shall hear it, He will answer thee." (Isaiah 30:19)

"The righteous cry, and the Lord heareth, and delivereth them out of all their troubles." (Psalm 34:17)

"In my distress I called upon the Lord, and cried unto my God: He heard my voice out of His temple, and my cry came before Him, even into His ears." (Psalm 18:6)

"The eyes of the Lord are upon the righteous, and His ears are open unto their cry." (Psalm 34:15)

"Hear my cry, O God; attend unto my prayer. From the end of the earth will I cry unto thee, when my heart is overwhelmed: lead me to the rock that is higher than I. For Thou hast been a shelter for me, and a strong tower from the enemy." (Psalm 61:1-3)

"In my distress I cried unto the Lord, and He heard me." (Psalm 120:1)

"And the Lord said, I have surely seen the affliction of My people which are in Egypt, and have heard their cry by reason of their taskmasters; for I know their sorrows; And I am come down to deliver them out of the hand of the Egyptians, and to bring them up out of that land unto a good land and a large, unto a land flowing with milk and honey; unto the place of the Canaanites, and the Hittites, and the Amorites, and the Perizzites, and the Hivites, and the Jebusites. Now therefore, behold, the cry of the children of Israel is come unto Me: and I have also seen the oppression wherewith the Egyptians oppress them." (Exodus 3:7-9)

God Will Never Forsake Us

"Sing, O heavens; and be joyful, O earth; and break forth into singing, O mountains: for the Lord hath comforted His people, and will have mercy upon His afflicted. But Zion said, The Lord hath forsaken me, and my Lord hath forgotten me. Can a woman forget her sucking child, that she should not have compassion on the son of her womb? yea, they may forget, yet will I not forget thee. Behold, I have graven thee upon the palms of My hands; thy walls are continually before Me." (Isaiah 49:13-16)

"For a small moment have I forsaken thee; but with great mercies will I gather thee. In a little wrath I hid My face from thee for a moment; but with everlasting kindness will I have mercy on thee, saith the Lord thy Redeemer." (Isaiah 54:7-8)

"Many are the afflictions of the righteous: but the Lord delivereth him out of them all." (Psalm 34:19)

"But the salvation of the righteous is of the Lord: He is their strength in the time of trouble. And the Lord shall help them, and deliver them: He shall deliver them from the wicked, and save them, because they trust in Him." (Psalm 37:39-40)

Courage

"Be strong and of a good courage, fear not, nor be afraid of them: for the Lord thy God, He it is that doth go with thee; He will not fail thee, nor forsake thee. And Moses called unto Joshua, and said unto him in the sight of all Israel, Be strong and of a good courage: for thou must go with this people unto the land which the Lord hath sworn unto their fathers to give them; and thou shalt cause them to inherit it. And the Lord, He it is that doth go before thee; He will be with thee, He will not fail thee, neither forsake thee: fear not, neither be dismayed." (Deuteronomy 31:6-8)

Peace

"The Lord will give strength unto His people; the Lord will bless His people with peace." (Psalm 29:11)

"Thou wilt keep him in perfect peace, whose mind is stayed on Thee: because he trusteth in Thee. Trust ye in the Lord for ever: for in the Lord Jehovah is everlasting strength." (Isaiah 26:3-4)

Feelings of Failure

"We have been with child, we have been in pain, we have as it were brought forth wind; we have not wrought any deliverance in the earth; neither have the inhabitants of the world fallen." (Isaiah 26:18)

Is it Worth Doing What is Right?

"Truly God is good to Israel, even to such as are of a clean heart. But as for me, my feet were almost gone; my steps had well nigh slipped. For I was envious at the foolish, when I saw the prosperity of the wicked. For there are no bands in their death: but their strength is firm. They are not in trouble as other men; neither are they plagued like other men. Therefore pride compasseth them about as a chain; violence covereth them as a garment. Their eyes stand out with fatness: they have more than heart could wish. They are corrupt, and speak wickedly concerning oppression: they speak loftily. They set their mouth against the heavens, and their tongue walketh through the earth. Therefore his people return hither: and waters of a full cup are wrung out to them. And they say, How doth God know? and is there knowledge in the most High? Behold, these are the ungodly, who prosper in the world; they increase in riches. Verily I have cleansed my heart in vain, and washed my hands in innocency. For all the day long have I been plagued, and chastened every

morning. If I say, I will speak thus; behold, I should offend against the generation of Thy children. When I thought to know this, it was too painful for me; Until I went into the sanctuary of God; then understood I their end. Surely Thou didst set them in slippery places: Thou castedst them down into destruction. How are they brought into desolation, as in a moment! they are utterly consumed with terrors. As a dream when one awaketh; so, O Lord, when Thou awakest, Thou shalt despise their image. Thus my heart was grieved, and I was pricked in my reins. So foolish was I, and ignorant: I was as a beast before Thee. Nevertheless I am continually with Thee: Thou hast holden me by my right hand. Thou shalt guide me with Thy counsel, and afterward receive me to glory. Whom have I in heaven but Thee? and there is none upon earth that I desire beside Thee. My flesh and my heart faileth: but God is the strength of my heart, and my portion for ever. For, lo, they that are far from Thee shall perish: Thou hast destroyed all them that go a whoring from Thee. But it is good for me to draw near to God: I have put my trust in the Lord God, that I may declare all Thy works." (Psalm 73)

Suffering

"For our light affliction, which is but for a moment, worketh for us a far more exceeding and eternal weight of glory; While we look not at the things which are seen, but at the things which are not seen: for the things which are seen are temporal; but the things which are not seen are eternal." (II Corinthians 4:17-18)

"We are troubled on every side, yet not distressed; we are perplexed, but not in despair; Persecuted, but not forsaken; cast down, but not destroyed. Always bearing about in the body the dying of the Lord Jesus, that the life also of Jesus might be made manifest in our body. For we which live are always delivered unto death for Jesus' sake, that the life also of Jesus might

293

be made manifest in our mortal flesh. So then death worketh in us, but life in you." (II Corinthians 4:8-12)

"My brethren, count it all joy when ye fall into divers temptations; Knowing this, that the trying of your faith worketh patience. But let patience have her perfect work, that ye may be perfect and entire, wanting nothing." (James 1:2-4)

"Forasmuch then as Christ hath suffered for us in the flesh, arm yourselves likewise with the same mind: for he that hath suffered in the flesh hath ceased from sin; That he no longer should live the rest of his time in the flesh to the lusts of men, but to the will of God." (I Peter 4:1-2)

"And we know that all things work together for good to them that love God, to them who are the called according to his purpose." (Romans 8:28)

The Story Behind "It Is Well with My Soul"

Have you heard the hymn, "It is Well with My Soul"? Have you ever wondered what circumstances caused those words to be penned?

A successful lawyer and businessman of Chicago, Horatio G. Spafford was married to Anna, and they had five children. They experienced tragedy in 1871 when their young son died of pneumonia and later that same year, lost much of their business in the great Chicago fire. Yet, through the mercy and kindness of God, their business flourished once again.

But, tragedy would strike another time. In November of 1873, Mrs. Spafford and their four daughters were on board the French ocean liner, Ville du Havre, sailing to Europe with over 300 passengers on board. Mr. Spafford had planned to sail with his family, but an unexpected business problem had arisen and he stayed behind to solve it, planning on joining them a few days later taking another ship. When the Ville du Havre had been at sea for about four days, it collided with the Loch Earn, a powerful, iron-hulled Scottish ship, causing all passengers to be in serious danger. Anna quickly brought their four daughters to the deck, knelt down and prayed with them. She asked that God would deliver them from this danger if that were His will, and if not, to make them willing to endure whatever His plan was. It was only 12 minutes before she knew the answer.

The Ville du Havre submerged beneath the waves of the Atlantic Ocean, carrying every one of the four Spafford children with it.

Anna was discovered by a sailor, who was rowing a small boat over the area where the ship had submerged. He rescued her, and another large ship picked them up nine days later, dropping them off in Cardiff, Wales. She sent a telegram message to her husband which began with the words, "Saved alone, what shall I do?" Later, one of the other survivors of the ship, Pastor Weiss, recalled the words of Anna, "God gave me four daughters. Now they have been taken from me. Someday I will understand why."

Immediately, Mr. Spafford booked passage on the next available ship to cross the waters and join his grieving wife. It is on this journey that he penned the words of this poem, according to Bertha Spafford Vester, a daughter born after the tragedy.

When peace like a river attendeth my way,

When sorrows like sea billows roll,

Whatever my lot, Thou hast taught me to say,

It is well, it is well with my soul.

It is well with my soul,

It is well, it is well with my soul!

The Lord granted them three more children, and once again, they experienced loss—at the age of four, one of those three children succumbed to the dreaded pneumonia and died. This story gave me hope in my grief. Here was a man who lost so much at once yet he could say, in the middle of his grief, that it was well with his soul. I pray that this story likewise encourages you, that no matter how many trials you have suffered, you can say with hope that it is well with your soul.

A Final Challenge

Dear grieving mother,

I have debated in my mind whether I should include what I am going to write in this chapter or not. This is something that can be a very sensitive issue, and it may seem like I am completely oblivious to your pain and the terror that you feel in your heart, but please be assured, I am not. As I pondered whether I should include this chapter, I felt that this was one of the key ingredients to my healing. I don't want to rob you of something that, even though it was terribly hard, helped me along my journey of healing. Please remember that I have had seven full-term pregnancies after the loss of Serena, and I have battled hard with this.

I know it is incredibly tempting to want to try to do everything within your power to prevent the same thing from happening again if you choose to try again after loss. Depending on your circumstances, your choices could be something like the following:

"I had a homebirth and it failed; I must deliver this next child in the hospital."

"I had a vaginal delivery and it failed; I must have a C-section this time."

"My baby's heartbeat stopped X amount of time before the due date, so we need to make sure this baby is out before that window of time comes."

"I am now considered a high-risk pregnancy (even though the medical system doesn't know why the baby died), so I have to have double the amount of tests, ultrasounds, etc."

While I would definitely want every effort to be made for your next little one to survive and be in your loving arms, I just want to encourage you to place your trust in the Lord and not in all of the steps that can be taken in an attempt to see your baby survive. When you understand that God is sovereign, you'll know that no matter what you try to do or control, it is ultimately up to Him. True peace only comes from completely surrendering to His will.

Just this past week, I was finding anxiety creeping into my heart and starting to give me that underlying agitated feeling in everything I was doing. I am at the "deathly silent" time (as I call it) in my pregnancy currently—that time period when the 1st-trimester symptoms of nausea and fatigue are going away, but I don't feel any movement yet. While I had just heard the baby's heartbeat last week, fear was still creeping in, trying to convince me that just maybe the heart was no longer beating this week. The distraction of thoughts in my mind made it hard to focus on anything else, and the joy of life was being sucked out of my being as I worried about something that may not even be a reality.

The anxiety was still stirring inside as I drove to Bible study, and as I listened to the lecture, it slowly began to dawn on me that once again, this pregnancy had become all about *my* desires, *my* hopes, *my* dreams, and *my* plans. The fear was arising because I was terrified that it would all come crashing down as it has in the past. And to be honest, I have no control over the outcome of this pregnancy or any pregnancy. My flesh would want to control the outcome with every part of my being, but I face the reality every single time that I am NOT in control. When I once again realized this as I drove home, I had a heart-to-heart conversation with the Lord.

"Lord, I am struggling with fear about this baby. I have no reason to fear that his or her life will end in miscarriage, but I am afraid. I have been focusing on *my* plans and hopes for this child. Help me to remember that this pregnancy is all about *Your* plans for this child, and that he or she is a gift from *You*. If Your plan for this child is to be a beacon of hope for those who lose their children, let me once again be a vessel in Your service. Please help me to surrender to Your will, whatever it may be, for this child."

It was only then that true peace washed over my soul. When I relinquished my grip on this child (don't hear me wrong, I'm not diminishing the amount of love I have for this unborn child), it was then that I experienced that calmness of spirit knowing that the Lord would only do that which is best for our family. I knew that He would give the grace to handle whatever plan He chose.

As I have spoken to bereaved mothers in the past, I have watched them struggle with the fear and the anxiety that I too have been plagued with. Just like me, they are seeking to find peace in extra tests, ultrasounds, doctors, and the medical system. My heart breaks for them because I know that all of those things and people cannot bring the deep, lasting peace that passes all understanding which our heart craves so much. It is only in surrendering our will to the Lord that we can experience that which our heart so desperately needs.

So, I want to challenge you, if you can manage that right now, to try to force yourself not to do that extra test, that extra ultrasound or make those extra appointments to try to prevent another devastating situation. For me, I chose to do another homebirth even though many would have thought I was crazy (or brave) to not go to the hospital. The reality is, I was far from brave and faltered in my faith so many times. Every morning, I had to fortify my mind with promises from the Scriptures, and I spent plenty of time crying out to the Lord with tears streaming down my cheeks. However, I felt that by facing those fears and not trying to set up what I (or others) would have thought was a perfect plan, my reliance upon the Lord was strengthened. It wasn't all about me, the midwife, the doctors or nurses or the hospital. It was all about God and His perfect plan, regardless of what it might be.

During that "deathly silent" time, I have often been tempted to go in for a "heartbeat check" to give me that reassurance that I so craved. But I quickly realized that even though the heart was beating at the time that I was at the appointment, it could stop the minute I walked out of the office. You see, we are totally and completely powerless over the life of our children. So, I, very falteringly, refused the temptation to merely try to put a Band-Aid on my wound—my fear that I would lose another baby and trying to control the outcome somehow—and resolved to face it head-on, allowing the Lord to heal from the depth of the wound and up to the surface.

I want to close this by reassuring you that if you are not at the place to take on this challenge, I completely understand. I don't condemn you. God takes each of us on our own particular path of healing, and each moves at a different pace. I just included this at the back of the book as a little challenge as I found it to be something that spurred me on in my journey of healing.

My prayer is that you will be inspired by my faltering faith to take hold of the Lord and find the peace that passes all understanding as you surrender the life of your child to His loving hands.

"And the peace of God, which passeth all understanding, shall keep your hearts and minds through Christ Jesus."

—Philippians 4:7

Acknowledgments

First, I want to acknowledge my Father in heaven who blessed me with Serena and gave me the gift of motherhood. You gave her to me, and You took her to be with You, and I can truly say, "Thank You, Father" for everything that You have taught me with my little girl's life and death. You have changed me into a woman that I would never have been without this deep suffering. Thank You for keeping me and holding me when I couldn't hold on. Thank You for picking me up when all I could do was crawl and drop myself at Your feet. Thank You for wrapping Your arms of love around me. Thank you for bottling up all of my tears and listening to my silent screams of pain. (Sometimes I wondered how You felt as You watched me writhe in pain during those dark nights.)

Thank You for wiping my tears away and giving me joy again. Thank You for being true to Your promises and making something beautiful out of my devastation. Thank You for being patient with all of my fears, doubts, anger, and lack of trust. Without You, I truly would not be here. Thank You for keeping me on the road that rainy, dreary night in October, where the rain was pouring outside on the highway, and my tears were raining on the inside of the Bravada. Thank You for keeping me and giving me the strength and grace to carry my cross when it was too hard to bear. Oh Lord,

I can't say enough how You have used Serena to bless me, my family and countless others. Thank You for not giving up on me when I couldn't understand Your plan and will. Thank You, Father, for keeping my baby (indeed, all of my babies) safe with You in heaven. Please hold her close tonight and give her a kiss for me. Whisper in her ear just how much I love her and that I am so thankful for what You have done in my life through her.

Thank You for helping me to write this book, giving me the grace to continue even when there were discouragements and "hiccups" along the way. Through Your Word and children, You encouraged me to "pull up my bootstraps" and finish this project so that others could be blessed. Thank You for once again proving that You help me to accomplish that which is completely impossible in my own human strength.

Next, I want to thank my husband, Elliott Neff, who was such a rock and anchor for me when we lost all of our babies. He patiently listened to all of my fears, doubts, and pointed me in the right direction. He supported me through all my tears and every emotion that I went through. He graciously endured all of my anxieties that I struggled with during subsequent pregnancies. And, he encouraged me to write this book.

I am abundantly blessed to have you as my husband, darling. I will never forget your strength and support during Serena's labor and delivery. You were there for me every step of the way. I will never forget the precious moments we had together during that long labor, working as a team to bring our baby into the world. Then, your tears when they saw on the ultrasound that she was gone, and your strength for me when I had to muster the courage to deliver Serena after she was dead.

Oh, darling, I am thankful she got to feel your hand on her head before she died. It always makes me smile with tears in my eyes. She had one of the most loving Daddies, and I think she knew it. Your unwavering faith in God was an inspiration when my faith was rocking, and I was crumbling inside. You loved me no matter how crazy my grief was, and I knew I could share whatever was on my heart and know that you still would love me. I can't tell you how much your unconditional love means to me, darling. I love you so much, and I always will.

My precious children here on this earth: Caleb Jeremiah (8.5), Nadine Renae (7), Joel Elioenai (6), Katrina Gabrielle (4.5), Enoch Andrew (3), Nathan Azariah (1.5) and our little one due in just a couple weeks. I am SO grateful that Jesus gave you to me. With each of your deliveries, I battled the fear of losing you, but Jesus gave me a peace that only comes with trusting in Him and being willing to surrender everything to His will. Every time I pushed one of you out and heard your cry, you have no idea what a beautiful sound that was to my ears as I never heard those sounds from your big sister.

Oh, dear ones, it blesses me to hear you talk about your big sister, and I am thankful that you have been exposed to some of these hard lessons from an early age. I pray that each of you would come to love and know Jesus as your Savior and Lord, so that one day, we will all be together, around Jesus' throne, worshipping Him forever and ever, never to say goodbye again. Thank you for the blessing that you are to me. My life has been, and continues to be, enriched by you. Thank you for your patience and those times where you all played outside harmoniously so Mommy could "work on her book." You will be a blessing to many others too.

I also want to thank my parents, Moses and Teletha Elossais, who labored tirelessly to train me up in the ways of the Lord. I would have never made it through these tragedies without knowing Jesus. Thank you for teaching me about Jesus' love and for teaching me the truth. Thank you for being good examples to me and hanging on to Jesus throughout the tough times you experienced.

Thank you, Mother, for being there the whole time I was in labor and being so supportive. I am so thankful that you got to hold her. The photos she has with you are among my favorites.

Thank you, Dad, for being real and letting your tears flow even though men often try to hide their tears. I still see you walking across the cemetery grass, carrying her little white casket with Elliott. I still see you being the next one after Elliott to lift the shovel and put dirt on her casket. I can't imagine what it was like for you and Mother, to know I was going through this when I was so far away from you. I am sure it was a test of faith for you too. I am truly blessed to have you as my parents.

I want to thank Holly Feenstra for sending me a letter and a poem when I miscarried our very first baby. You were an excellent example to me of reaching out to someone who is undergoing the same trial that you walked through. I am fairly shy, and I would have never dreamed of messaging couples who I don't know, who live across the country or on the other side of the world, but your stepping out and doing that for me inspired me to do it for others. The count must be over forty now, including miscarried little ones. Holly, please know that your act of service to Christ has been multiplied.

I want to acknowledge Mrs. Deborah Alderliesten, Aunt Sharon Reimers, and Colleen Catterall. Each of these women lost a baby in the womb years before I lost Serena and they served as a beacon of hope when I was brought so low with grief. Seeing them living vibrant Christian lives after losing a child encouraged me that it **was** possible.

I want to thank the people at Made for Success Publishing, who were willing to take on this project. Thank you for all your assistance and guidance in bringing this book into being, helping me minister to those who are bowed down with grief.

Thank you also to my ed

itor, Katie, for all of the effort and time she put into helping this manuscript become what it is.

Thank you to my mother, siblings, and friends for sharing their thoughts on titles and graphics, helping me come to a final decision.

Many thanks to my youngest brother, Manuel Elossais, who at 15 years of age, assisted me in writing the author bio—a daunting task for me—as well as offering intelligent wording when my brain was too saturated.

Last, but not least, I want to acknowledge the many mothers who the Lord brought into my life over the past ten years whose babies also were given "express tickets" to heaven. I have learned much from them and developed special friendships.

1. *Sarita Joy Feenstra,* daughter of Mark and Bethany Feenstra -August 19, 2009

2. *Alexandra Jo Barnhill,* daughter of Dan and Kolleen Barnhill - September 30, 2009

3. Benjamin and Kim Beaudoin's baby

4. *Ava Sophia Terlouw,* daughter of Alex and Vanessa Terlouw - April 9, 2009 - October 17, 2009 (unexpected death during sleep)

5. *Ella Marie Mowery-* daughter of Alex and Amy Mowery - May 5, 2010

6. Titus Gershom Liddle, son of Ian and Amanda Liddle - March 11, 2011 (20-weeks gestation)

7. *Levi Wrangler Lee,* son of Cameron and Sarah Lee - June 2, 2012 (23 weeks gestation)

8. *Mahalani Lucy Prussic,* daughter of Tim and Maile Prussic - December 3, 2012

9. *Isabella Joy Canciglia,* daughter of Michael and Marjie Canciglia - April 25, 2013

10. *Kendrah Grace Isitt,* daughter of Joe and Sarah Isitt and granddaughter of David and Kimberly Stelzer - July 18, 2013

11. *Isaac Levi Parr,* Son of Jacob and Brittany Parr - October 4, 2013

12. *Arpan S.,* son of Shawn and Sophiya S. - October 18, 2013

13. *Elijah M,* son of Isaac and Rachel M. - March 2014

14. *Judah Daniel Zwicker,* son of Tim and Elizabeth Zwicker - May 4, 2014

15. *Britton Ione Ishmael,* daughter of Jon and Jenny Ishmael - May 7, 2014

16. *Allie Rae Mowery,* daughter of Alex and Amy Mowery - July 3, 2014

17. *Malachi Englefield,* son of Peter and Michelle Englefield - May 7, 2011 - September 4, 2015 (complex medical issues)

18. *Shepherd Felmley,* son of Kyle and Karen Felmley - September 27, 2015 (20 weeks gestation)

19. *Son of C. Doyle,* died during sleep in March 2016

20. *Brynn Ruth Key,* daughter of Tim and Lacey Key - December 2, 2015 - April 17, 2016 (unexpected death during sleep)

21. *Colton B.,* son of Jon and Lesley B. - December 2015- May 13, 2016 (unexpected death during sleep)

22. *Ian James Isitt,* son of Joe and Sarah Isitt - September 27, 2016 - October 16, 2016

23. *Isaiah Neff,* son of Raphael and Joanna Neff - December 9, 2016 (16 weeks gestation)

24. *Isabella Claire Biersgreen,* daughter of Arlen and Elizabeth Biersgreen. - June 9-10, 2017

25. *Marceline Abigail Fouard,* daughter of Jean-Michel and Wendie Fouard - July 24, 2017

26. *Eleanor Hilda Smart,* twin daughter of Jeremy and Andrea Smart- August 21, 2017 - August 23, 2017

27. *Simon Alexander Y.,* son of Nathan and Kathryn Y. - September 4, 2017

28. *Kirk C.,* son of Mark and Belinda C. - September 2017

- October 2017 (5 months gestation)

29. *Julia Jo Arns*, daughter of John and Brianna Arns - March 6, 2018 (28 weeks gestation)

30. *James Daniel Soderna*, son of James and Alanna Soderna - July 19, 2018

31. Miscarried little ones: Baby Baldwin, Baby Beaudoin, Baby Betchel, Baby "Raphael" Beukema, Babies Dzuiba, Babies Feenstra, Baby "Reliance" Felmey, Baby Hansen, Baby Herstad, Babies Ishmael, Baby McMillan, Babies Neff, Baby Remington, Babies Shedrock, Baby Sinding, Babies Small, Baby Smoots, and many other little ones who took their "flight" early on in pregnancy.

(taken on May 31, 2018)

(Nadine, Camilla holding Nathan, Elliott, holding Enoch with Serena's bear, Katrina, Caleb and Joel)

About The Author

When Camilla's first baby girl, Serena, died unexpectedly during labor, her soul was crushed and her faith was challenged. But as the Lord healed her heart, He brought other bereaved mothers into her life by the dozens. It slowly became clear that He had blessed her with a message she needed to share: there is hope after such devastation.

Camilla Neff is the wife of Elliott, and blessed mother of their brood of wonderful children. Having been blessed with 11 pregnancies, she has experienced 3 miscarriages and 1 stillbirth. Camilla is grateful that the Lord has filtered these trials through His fingers of love, fulfilling His promise of bringing beauty out of ashes. Camilla lives in Seattle, spending her time nurturing and homeschooling their precious children, supporting her husband as a business owner and bringing hope and healing to others.